Transforming Fell and Valley

Landscape and Parliamentary Enclosure in North West England

Ian Whyte

Centre for North-West Regional Studies
University of Lancaster
2003
Series Editor: Jean Turnbull

Transforming Fell and Valley

This volume is the 49th in a series published by the
Centre for North-West Regional Studies at the University of Lancaster

Designed, typeset, printed and bound by
JW Arrowsmith Ltd, Bristol

British Library Cataloguing-in-Publication Data
A CIP catalogue record for this book is available from the British Library

ISBN 1-86220-132-3

Contents

List of Illustrations

Maps

Figures

List of Tables

Acknowledgements

I would like to express my gratitude to the staff of the record offices in Preston, Kendal and Barrow for their assistance and patience, to Chris Beacock for producing the maps, and to Jean Turnbull and Angus Winchester for reading the text and offering invaluable comments and suggestions.

Abbreviations

The abbreviations below are used to locate the areas of various enclosure awards within their pre-1974 counties:

Cu	Cumberland
La	Lancashire
Yo	Yorkshire
We	Westmorland

The following abbreviations relate to archives:

CRO	Cumbria Record Office
LRO	Lancashire Record Office

Other abbreviations used in the text:

Ha	Hectares
OS	Ordnance Survey
TCWAAS	Transactions of the Cumberland and Westmorland Antiquarian and Archaeological Society

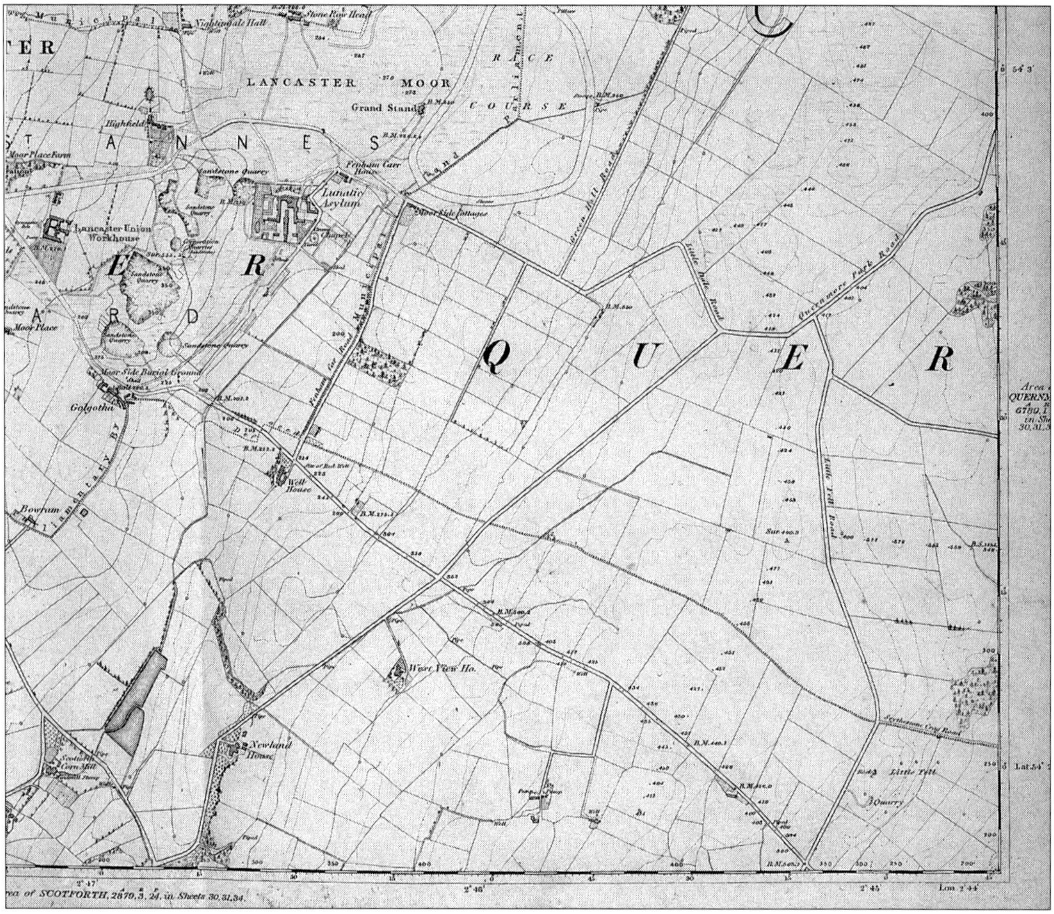

Frontispiece: This extract from the first edition of the Ordnance Survey six-inch map for Quernmore shows the classic regular landscape associated with parliamentary enclosure. Reproduced courtesy of Lancaster University Library.

CHAPTER ONE

Introduction

Although extensive areas of open common grazings still exist in the uplands of the north west, many fells, and the marginal country around their fringes, are broken up by patterns of field boundaries, access roads, farmsteads and other features which have a neat, orderly appearance (Frontispiece, Figure 1). At their most extreme such areas can have a painfully regular geometry of square fields and roads intersecting at right angles, sometimes ignoring the detail of the topography in their quest for regularity (Figure 2). Their uphill boundary with open moorland, or sometimes along a watershed with an adjoining, unenclosed common, may be marked by a striking contrast in vegetation between the bright green of improved grassland within the fields and dark heather moorland or pale acid grassland outside them. Lower down, the junction between the large square or rectangular fields and smaller, much less regularly-shaped older enclosures is often just as prominent on the map or in the landscape. The contrast between large, regular allotments high on the fellsides and smaller irregularly-shaped enclosures lower down is striking if you stand on a hillside overlooking Dentdale or Garsdale (Yo) and look across to the opposite side of the valley (Figure 3). The boundary is a wavy line, marking the former head dyke, or limit of improvement, in the mid-eighteenth century along the edge of what was once the common pasture before the newer, larger allotments were created.

The planned appearance of such landscapes can be striking even when travelling past them rapidly on the motorway: over Shap, on the fringes of Bowland, passing Lancaster, or crossing Stainmore on the A66 for instance. If you are driving on country roads you may experience an abrupt transition at the boundary between old enclosed land and areas of newer fields. One minute you may be driving on a narrow, winding road, hemmed in by hedges and overhung by trees. Then suddenly the road widens out, becoming completely straight with broad verges, rich in wild flowers, while the view also opens out. Just as suddenly, you may come to a characteristic right-angled bend in the road and have to slow right down to negotiate it. Often the land within the fields on either side of you will have been improved. Today it is more likely to be under pasture rather than crops but with the light of a low-slanting evening or winter sun you can often pick out the straight, parallel corrugations of former

Figure 1: A regular pattern of large, square parliamentary enclosure fields on the edge of Inglewood Forest, north of Penrith.

Figure 2: Dufton Fell – the enclosure walls ignore minor topographic features in order to maintain a regular plan. Reproduced by kind permission of A.J.L. Winchester.

Figure 3: The contrast between the large, regular fields of the parliamentary enclosure era on the upper slopes of Dentdale and the small, irregular ones of earlier date on the lower slopes is striking.

ridge-and-furrow ploughing, indicating cultivation from before the days of mass-produced pipes for underground tile drains. In other cases the vegetation in the fields may be indistinguishable from that on nearby open moorland, suggesting that, if the land was ever improved, it must have occurred a long time ago and possibly only for a brief period.

The OS 1:25,000 maps sometimes distinguish some of the larger of these regular fields with names like 'Lord's Lot' or 'Bishop's Tithe Allotment', suggesting that some kind of share-out of land has occurred in the past. These efficiently-planned landscapes are areas of parliamentary enclosure. Under the authority of acts of Parliament former common land, which in the north west was mainly rough pasture, was divided up among those people who had rights to use it, mainly for grazing but also for a range of other activities. In the process the commons were extinguished, the former commoners receiving specific blocks of land, or allotments, in lieu of their original common rights. The creation of the new enclosed landscape was overseen by Parliament through an act for each manor, parish or township. In this process, which operated between the later eighteenth and later nineteenth centuries, the landscapes of extensive areas of the north west were profoundly transformed. The landscapes created by parliamentary enclosure have often changed relatively little since then. Some of the land enclosed by parliamentary act in the north west – a very small proportion – involved remnants of open-field arable land. Some of it consisted of valley meadows and peat mosses, lowland commons and coastal salt marshes, but the bulk of it was upland pasture.

People often fail to realise how extensive, and how recent, this landscape revolution was. The slopes of many of the region's best-known fells, like High Street or Whernside, often thought of as really wild country, have been carefully evaluated, mapped and parcelled out by the enclosure commissioners and their surveyors.

Parliamentary enclosure is a process which many people vaguely remember hearing about at school. Often there is a general perception of the process being driven by major landowners, with small farmers, cottagers and squatters being disadvantaged or even driven out. There were, in fact, two main types of parliamentary enclosure; first open-field arable land, mainly in the midlands, eastern and southern England, and second common pasture and waste, some of it in the lowlands but the bulk of it in northern England and Wales.[1] A lot of the research on parliamentary enclosure has focused on the first category; much less is known about the enclosure of upland commons. Within the north west there have been some detailed individual case studies[2] but no broad overview; many aspects of the process, and the landscape it created, are poorly understood. Over England and Wales as a whole, parliamentary enclosure began to gather momentum in the 1760s reaching a peak during the Napoleonic Wars and tailing off by the mid-nineteenth century.[3] Estimates of the total amount of land involved vary between 6.7 and 7.25 million acres (2.6–2.9 million ha) in England or 8.4 million acres (3.4 million ha) if Wales is included: about 24 per cent of the total area of land of which some 2.3 million acres (0.9 million ha) were common pasture rather than open-field arable, much of it in the uplands.[4] These figures are not precise because the award documents prepared by the enclosure commissioners for each parish, manor or township, the most important of the historical sources relating to parliamentary enclosure, are not always precise about how much land was involved.

Notes

1. M. Turner, *English Parliamentary Enclosure: its historical geography and economic history* (Dawson, 1980).
2. For example, R.S. Dilley 'The case of the Stainton, Newbiggin and Blencow enclosure award', *TCWAAS*, Series 2, 95 (1995), pp.187–98; N. Gregson, 'Tawney revisited: custom and the emergence of capitalist class relations in north east Cumbria 1600–1830', *Economic History Review* 42 (1) (1989), pp.18–42.
3. Turner, *Parliamentary Enclosure.*
4. G.E. Mingay, *Parliamentary Enclosure in England: an introduction to its causes, incidence and impact, 1750–1850* (Longman, 1998), p.12.

CHAPTER TWO

The background to parliamentary enclosure

1. *The countryside before parliamentary enclosure*

In the early years of the eighteenth century Daniel Defoe, travelling through the north west, was not impressed with the landscape. He described Westmorland as 'the wildest, most barren and frightful of any (county) that I have passed over in England, or even in Wales'.[1] He viewed the hill country of the north west as 'all barren and wild, of no use nor advantage either to man or beast' with the valleys between being almost as bleak and inhospitable.[2] By the end of the 1760s the appearance of the countryside had not changed much. Arthur Young, the agricultural improver, travelling between Keswick and Penrith, found most of the countryside uncultivated moorland though capable of improvement. The road from Shap to Kendal passed through another huge tract of moorland 'melancholy to behold' yet with soil that was capable of cultivation.[3] The Cumbrian region had the highest proportion of unenclosed upland waste of any region of England in the later eighteenth century. As late as 1800, when parliamentary enclosure was already well under way, the proportions of the area of Westmorland, Cumberland and Lancashire accounted for by waste was 79.7 per cent, 50.5 per cent and 9.0 per cent respectively, though the figure for north Lancashire was much higher than the county as a whole.[4]

In the first half of the eighteenth century many parts of the north west's countryside had the appearance of small islands of enclosed and improved land surrounded by a sea of unimproved waste. In the lower part of the Lune valley the strip of improved land was, in places, only a mile wide, with moorland running down to the outskirts of Lancaster (Map 1). In the wooded limestone country around Arnside and Silverdale most of the craggy hills and many of the peaty valley floors were still common pasture with only narrow strips of improved land and settlement between. Some villages, such as Murton (We) below Cross Fell, still had remnants of their medieval open fields though in most cases they had already been enclosed by private agreements between their cultivators often leaving fossilised traces of the former open-field strips in

long, narrow strip fields with gently curving boundaries.[5] Beyond the villages and their fields lay scattered farmsteads and cottages set among areas of small, irregularly-shaped hedged and walled fields, referred to by the later enclosure commissioners as 'old' or 'ancient' enclosures (Figure 4).

Figure 4: Irregular pattern of 'old enclosures' from the pre-parliamentary enclosure era, North Stainmore.

Map 1 (*opposite*): Part of Yates' map of Lancashire 1786 showing the extent of unimproved waste in the lower Lune valley in the later eighteenth century. Reproduced courtesy of Lancaster University Library.

Some of these were late-medieval in date but some were more recent squatter intakes from the common pastures. Beyond these stretched the commons, former manorial wastes, in many cases medieval hunting forests which had been opened up for grazing, gradually being appropriated by the tenants of individual manors.[6] In many cases these commons ran right down into the villages as funnel-shaped driftways for moving livestock, opening out from village greens, as at Maulds Meaburn, Great Musgrave or Winton (We). In long, straggling villages like Troutbeck (We) each farm had its own access way or *outrake* on to the commons. The edge of the moor, along local roads, was sometimes marked by place names like 'Moor Gate'. Farmsteads were frequently located near the edges of commons and lines of them along the old boundaries of the commons can still be picked out on the modern map.

The commons were criss-crossed by networks of roads, tracks and footpaths, some linking communities on either side, some more local in their purpose such as tracks for bringing sled loads of peat down to individual farms (Map 2). In the mouths of the driftways, where they opened out on to the commons, and elsewhere on the lower slopes of the fells, groups of farmers, with the permission of the lords of their manors, had often taken in areas of common pasture and enclosed them with ring fences as stinted pastures in which specific numbers of animals could be grazed, shared between only a few people rather than by all the

commoners. These pastures were mainly used seasonally for grazing animals between late autumn and early spring.[7] Some of these cow pastures, or *cowbounds* as they were often called, may have been created as early as the fifteenth century but others were established as late as the nineteenth century. At a later date they were sometimes divided into

Map 2: Part of Jeffreys' Map of Westmorland 1770 showing the dense patterns of trackways across the commons south of Appleby.

separate allotments, rather than stints, by parliamentary acts, as with Ellergill, Langdale and Roundthwaite cowbounds in the upper Lune valley; or alternatively they were incorporated into the areas of larger enclosure awards.

The existence of these enclosed stinted pastures and of the early fields around settlements emphasises that enclosure was not solely a phenomenon of the eighteenth and nineteenth centuries. Nor was all the enclosure carried out at this period accomplished with the aid of parliamentary acts. Enclosure involved two principal elements: first the removal of communal rights from an area of land, whether arable, meadow or pasture, and its replacement by the management of a single owner. Second was the surrounding of the land by a clearly-demarcated boundary fence. Enclosure of common land had been going on since the Middle Ages. As has been mentioned above, strips in the open fields surrounding villages in Cumberland, Westmorland and Lancashire were consolidated into blocks and surrounded by hedges through private agreements between groups of farmers. In addition, areas of common pasture were nibbled away through individual encroachments by local people and incoming squatters, especially during the early seventeenth century when population was rising steadily.[8] Before the eighteenth century agreements to enclose land out of open fields or to create stinted pastures must often have been verbal ones approved by local manorial courts. By the eighteenth century written agreements were being drawn up and the process of dividing out the land prior to putting boundaries round it was being undertaken by one or more arbiters, local men, but ones who did not have any direct interest in the land involved and who could be seen to be acting impartially. They were forerunners of the commissioners appointed by Parliament to undertake the work of enclosure.

Commons formed an important resource for the inhabitants of upland fringe communities. As well as providing grazing they were also a source of building stone. In the neighbourhood of Lancaster quarrying for building stone and millstones on Quernmore common was widespread.[9] Coal, lead, copper and iron were also worked. In addition, commons were major sources of fuel in the form of peat and sometimes gorse and wood. Turf and heather were used for walling and roofing, bracken was cut for bedding in stables and cowsheds. The exploitation of these resources was regulated in the interest of the community by local manorial courts which, down to the early eighteenth century, appear to have functioned reasonably effectively.

The grazing rights of individuals on the commons were regulated in various ways. Sometimes they were *sans nombre*, where landholders could graze as many animals on the common in summer as they could winter on their improved *in-bye* land. In other cases commons were divided into *stints* or *cattlegates* which were allocated proportionally in relation to the amount of improved in-bye land held by each commoner. The former was more frequent in the Lake District, the latter in the Pennines.[10] On some commons, when a landholder was not grazing his full quota of animals his rights could be *agisted* or leased to graziers from outside the community. By the mid-eighteenth century this was becoming increasingly frequent with the rise of the droving trade in lean cattle southwards from Scotland, providing the growing northern industrial towns and London with fresh meat. Increasingly, common rights were being abused as stints were exceeded or too many agisted animals brought in, leading to overgrazing and damage to the pastures. The Cartmel commons, at the time of the enclosure act in 1796, were said to have been grazed bare due to overstocking.[11] The larger farmers especially were increasingly prepared to defy the manorial courts, whose powers were rapidly weakened.[12] The only feasible course of action, many landowners considered, was to enclose the commons so that they could manage their individual shares more effectively. In addition, many commons were being reduced in size due to encroachments. Where commons were extensive, manorial courts often permitted this. In Cartmel in 1757, 75 landholders in the parish were accused of appropriating 84 parcels of land in this way. They were each allowed to keep the land they had taken in return for a payment to the parish vestry.[13] The money was paid into an 'encroachment fund' the interest from which was divided among the local poor.[14] But Cartmel had the advantage of over 12,000 acres (4,856ha) of common land so that such losses were not as great a problem as in parishes and townships where the extent of common grazings was much smaller. In some instances manorial courts, lords of manors and their stewards agreed to piecemeal enclosure as a means of reducing poverty and cutting the poor rates. In Warton parish (La) in 1740 it was agreed by all the freehold and customary tenants to enclose a part of the common called The Miers and stint it to provide grazing and hay for poor cottagers in the parish.[15]

So enclosure of land from the common waste had been continuing on a small scale for centuries. Parliamentary enclosure was only the last of a long series of processes in which rights to the use of land were defined increasingly clearly and carefully.[16] In late-medieval times manorial lords had created *vaccaries*, large cattle farms, under their own direct management, in their hunting forests. Other areas of forest and waste were opened up for peasant settlement with the establishment of clusters of small holdings.[17] During the late sixteenth and early seventeenth centuries the renewed build up of population led to many people squatting on commons and improving small areas of land round the fringes of Bowland and the Lake District and in Pennine valleys.[18] During the seventeenth century it was possible to have a more official seal of approval stamped on such proceedings by taking them to the Court of Chancery, though only a few such cases from north west England are known.[19] By the mid-eighteenth century privately-agreed enclosure proceedings were becoming more formalised and it was recognised that a more structured way was needed to enclose larger areas. Obtaining an act of Parliament to confirm an enclosure process was first used in 1604 for Radipole in Dorset but became much more popular from the 1760s as population growth became more rapid, food prices rose and the need for agricultural improvement became more evident. In all 5,265 separate English enclosure acts were passed by 1914.[20] Enclosure could still be achieved by private agreement and when all the parties concerned were in favour of enclosure this was a much cheaper procedure, but appeal to Parliament allowed landowners with a majority share in the land concerned to push ahead with enclosure despite unenthusiastic neighbours. Between the 1770s and the later nineteenth century it became the main process for enclosing upland commons in north west England. It was the most rapid and extensive form of enclosure and had a marked impact on the landscape.

2. *Historical sources for parliamentary enclosure*

Although this study looks at parliamentary enclosure throughout north Lancashire and Cumbria, much of the detail is taken from an analysis of the enclosure awards and related documents for the old counties of Westmorland and Lancashire from the Forest of Bowland northwards, including Furness and Cartmel. What we know about the processes and effects of parliamentary enclosure derives mainly from a limited range of documentary sources. The initial bills, or petitions, submitted to Parliament requesting that an enclosure act be passed may survive in manuscript or printed form among collections of estate and solicitors' papers. The published *House of Commons Journal* can be used to follow the progress of bills through various readings in Parliament and also, sometimes, to provide evidence of opposition to enclosure. Petitions against a bill or other documents, such as accounts of the expenses of the petitioners, also survive in some cases.

In total, 127 enclosure acts were passed for Cumberland, 98 for Westmorland and 31 for north Lancashire, although some of these involved lowland rather than upland areas. The printed acts of Parliament relating to enclosure survive more widely than the original bills. Solicitors and estate stewards sometimes preserved collections relating to particular districts and many of these have been deposited in county record offices. The acts for each county, listed chronologically and giving the amount and type of land involved, have been summarised in a Domesday of enclosures.[21] Until 1801 enclosure was achieved through individual private acts of Parliament. Although printed enclosure acts are fairly standardised in structure and format their wording varies in detail, especially in the case of acts from before the General Enclosure Act of 1801.

The most important documents of all were the enclosure awards, and their associated maps which detailed the decisions of the commissioners regarding how the area of land concerned should be divided up and allocated. Earlier awards from the later eighteenth century were generally written on large sheets of parchment, usually stuck together and rolled up with the award map. For larger areas of enclosure these documents can sometimes be the size of a small carpet and are difficult to hold down on an archive table; you can spend as much time fighting them as reading them! Some awards, such as the one for Cartmel (La), were bound, together with the accompanying maps, into large leather-covered volumes. Others were just roughly folded. The award documents themselves are written in continuous script, without paragraph divisions, often in awkward handwriting and always in convoluted legal prose. This makes them difficult to read although modern typed transcripts are available in a few cases. Early awards, such as Ellel (La) from 1756, are more variable in structure and content. Although they are generally fairly standard in format, like the acts whose wording they echo, awards vary considerably in detail emphasising that, despite the oversight of Parliament, they were essentially local products designed to meet local conditions and needs.[22] Several copies of awards and their maps were generally made. One copy was supposedly lodged with local Justices of the Peace and most of these survive among the Quarter Sessions material in county record offices. Copies were also kept with the parish records, while others were retained by local landed families and in solicitors' offices. Despite this in some cases – like Aughton (La) and Dufton, Preston Patrick and Great Strickland (We) – no known award has survived while in other instances, such as Ellel (La), there are no maps. In such circumstances estate maps and other documents sometimes allow the boundaries of an enclosed area to be determined. Awards from the early nineteenth century onwards generally list the allotments awarded to individual landholders in a table. For earlier awards these details are recorded as part of the continuous text and are more tedious to extract although they are often summarised in the margins or on the award map. After 1845, when enclosure processes were overseen by a permanent commission based in London and local commissioners became known as valuers, awards became much shorter and less convoluted in style, but also less informative.

The processes of enclosure, before an award was made, generated a range of documents, including handbills and newspaper advertisements for the various public meetings organised by the commissioners, details of the perambulations of the boundaries of commons, written claims to common rights, manuscript or printed notices of the award of allotments, contracts for making lengths of walling and stretches of roads, and general correspondence. The activities of the commissioners are sometimes recorded in minute books, and the costs incurred totalled in account books but, unlike the awards, commissioners were not required to preserve such material. In making a valuation of the land held by each commoner they often conducted surveys of the old enclosures but these have rarely survived. Disputes arising from enclosure proceedings – over the boundaries of commons for example – were considered by local Quarter Sessions and turn up in their records. In addition, a variety of material including the comments of agricultural improvers, topographical accounts, trade directories and census data may help to throw light on the processes of parliamentary enclosure, the rural society which it affected, and the landscape that it created.

Notes

1. D. Defoe, *A Tour Through the Whole Island of Great Britain* (Penguin 1971, originally published 1724–26), p.550.
2. Defoe, *Tour,* p.549.
3. A. Young, *A Six Months Tour Through the North of England* (Kelley 1967, originally published 1771), pp.108, 131.
4. M. Williams, 'The enclosure and reclamation of waste land in England and Wales in the eighteenth and nineteenth centuries', *Institute of British Geographers Transactions,* 51 (1970), pp.55–69.
5. B. Tyson, 'Murton Great Field near Appleby: a case-study of the piecemeal enclosure of a common field in the mid-eighteenth century', *TCWAAS,* Series 2, 92 (1992), pp.161–82.
6. A.J.L. Winchester, 'Dividing lines in a moorland landscape: territorial boundaries in upland England', *Landscapes* 1 (2) (2000), pp.16–32.
7. A. Fleming, *Swaledale, Valley of the Wild River* (Edinburgh University Press, 1998), p.74.
8. A.B. Appleby, *Famine in Tudor and Stuart England* (Liverpool University Press, 1978), pp.34–36, 60–61.
9. P. Hudson, 'Quarrying and extractive industries', in M. Winstanley (ed.) *Rural Industries of the Lune Valley* (CNWRS, 2000), pp.41–56.
10. A.J.L. Winchester, *The Harvest of the Hills: rural life in Northern England and the Scottish Borders, 1400–1700* (Edinburgh University Press, 2000), p.80.
11. J. Stockdale, *Annals of Cartmel* (Kitchin, 1872), p.326.
12. C.E. Searle, 'Customary tenants and the enclosure of the Cumbrian commons', *Northern History* 29, (1993), pp.126–53.
13. Stockdale, *Cartmel,* pp.197–8.
14. *Ibid.,* p. 235.
15. LRO PR 2768/2.

16. Winchester, *Harvest*, p.26.
17. A.J.L. Winchester, *Landscape and Society in Medieval Cumbria* (John Donald, 1987), pp.38–44.
18. Appleby, *Famine*, pp.344–36, 60–6; J. Porter, *The Making of the Central Pennines* (Moorland, 1980), pp.29–41.
19. S. Hollowell, *Enclosure Records for Historians* (Phillimore, 2000), pp.1–3.
20. M.E. Turner, *English Parliamentary Enclosure: its historical geography and economic history* (Dawson, 1980), p.18.
21. W.E. Tate (ed), *A Domesday of English Enclosure Awards* (University of Reading, 1978).
22. J. Chapman, 'Some problems in the interpretation of enclosure awards', *Agricultural History Review* 26 (1978), pp.108–114.

CHAPTER THREE

Patterns of parliamentary enclosure

1. *The environmental background*

Within the uplands of north west England there is great diversity of topography and landscape. Even within the Lake District the three main geological divisions give rise to areas with markedly different upland landscapes. The Skiddaw Slates in the north produce high but rounded fells with few rock outcrops. The Borrowdale Volcanics in the centre create much rougher, more rugged, craggy terrain. The Silurian strata in the south of the area give rise to lower rolling hill country on either side of Windermere. Facing the Lake District is the steep scarp face and peaty plateaux of the Cross Fell range and the north Pennines. A curving band of limestone forming a series of plateaux and valleys, stretching from Shap to Kirkby Stephen, offered considerable scope for agricultural improvement. South of this lie the flat-topped but steep-sided Howgill Fells. More limestone hills are found around Sedbergh, Dentdale and Garsdale, and further southwards at lower altitudes, between Kirkby Stephen and the Lune valley and in the Arnside-Silverdale area. South of the Lune the gritstone Bowland fells are acid and covered with extensive areas of blanket peat. Between these uplands are valleys and coastal lowlands with more fertile soils, particularly in the Eden valley draining to the Solway and, to a less marked extent, in the lower Lune valley and west Cumberland, while around Morecambe Bay were extensive areas of lowland peat moss and salt marsh ripe for reclamation. In many places though, as with the country north and east of Kendal, or around Cockermouth, the lowlands are broken up by ridges which, although not high and impressive, were still unimproved in the later eighteenth century.

All these areas were used as common pasture: all of them had potential for enclosure and improvement. However, this potential varied considerably with climate and soil conditions. In a maritime climate like that of north west England, as experienced fell walkers are well aware, quite modest gains in altitude can lead to a dramatic deterioration in climatic conditions. The amount of sunshine, the average temperature and the length of the growing season falls rapidly with altitude while windspeeds, cloudiness, rainfall and the amount of moisture in the soil increases. The climate, together with topography and both the solid and drift geology, are major influences on the character of soils. In areas like the Eden valley, west Cumbria and the Lune valley many of the soils at lower altitudes which underlay late eighteenth-century commons were potentially quite fertile if drained properly and cultivated using suitable rotations. However, the soils in many areas, such as those which underlay the extensive Forest of Inglewood (Cu), enclosed from 1819, were heavy, cold, wet clays developed on glacial tills which tended to deteriorate if not treated carefully, soils which tended to poach under the hooves of animals or become compacted by machinery.[1] At a local scale, soils could vary markedly over short distances. Sometimes this was due to topography, as in the lowlands south of Kendal or in the Eden valley where long oval-shaped mounds of glacial drift, or drumlins, had free-draining soils on their crests and slopes, with waterlogged soils in the hollows between. Sometimes the nature of the rocks below caused marked changes in soil conditions, as around Drybeck (We) where soils above the Triassic sandstones are better drained and easier to work than the clays above the Carboniferous limestone, causing marked differences in the potential of the soil for cultivation even within the same farm. In the upper Eden valley, the country around Kendal and Morecambe Bay and in parts of west Cumbria, thin soils over limestone were well drained and potentially fertile but vulnerable to over-cultivation. On the high plateaux, soils developed on peat were barely fit to improve at all, even as pasture.

So prospects for improvement varied greatly between one area of high ground and the next. The date at which an area was enclosed, even whether it was ever enclosed at all, depended partly on differences in altitude, climate, geology, topography, soil quality and drainage. However, environmental conditions aside, the location of the area, the quality of its transport links, the social structure of its communities, the pattern of landownership, the nature of the local economy and individual initiative were also powerful influences on enclosure history, producing patterns which are complex and not always easy to explain. The fact that an area of land had been enclosed and was under individual rather than communal management, meant that temporary improvement during periods of high prices and great demand such as the Napoleonic or Second World Wars, was always a possibility.

2. *The legislative context*

Until 1801 groups of landowners wishing to enclose a common or area of open-field arable land had to petition Parliament for a private act. This was a time-consuming process, particularly the drafting of the initial bill, the expense of which may often have delayed enclosure or even discouraged it from taking place at all. By the end of the eighteenth century agricultural writers were stressing the need for a general enclosure act which would speed up the parliamentary process and reduce costs substantially. What was actually passed in 1801 as a General Enclosure Act disappointed many people and was seen as a failure. Under the act suitable standard clauses from previous enclosure acts which had proved useful from past experience were identified and incorporated into a standardised blueprint for future legislation. Enclosure by private act continued but the process of drawing up a bill which eventually became an act was streamlined so that the initial stages of the process should not have taken so much time and ought to have cost correspondingly less. Agricultural writers continued to clamour for a proper general enclosure act which would do away with the need for separate private acts for each parish or township. In 1836 an act was passed which allowed enclosure to take place without reference to Parliament if two-thirds of the proprietors, in terms of value of property rather than numbers, were in agreement. If seven-eighths of them were in favour of enclosure they could proceed without the appointment of a commissioner. This act only covered open-field arable but a number of such remnants in valleys like Kentmere (We), Langdale (We) and Threlkeld (Cu) were enclosed under its provisions. An act of 1840 extended the provisions of this act to the enclosure of commons. In 1845 a more thorough reform was undertaken when a standing committee for enclosure was set up, based in London. Proposals for enclosure were submitted to the committee who appointed a local commissioner, or 'valuer' to undertake the task. They were required to produce shorter, less complex awards than the previous commissioners. At this stage Parliament still considered that a substantial proportion of the remaining commons, even in the uplands, were improvable and it was hoped that this procedure would considerably reduce the costs of enclosure and encourage land reclamation.[2] Of the enclosure awards for Cumbria and north Lancashire, 17 per cent were passed as private acts before 1801, 45 per cent between 1801 and 1845, 8 per cent under the acts of 1836 and 1840, and 30 per cent under the 1845 act.[3]

By 1876 there was less pressure to enclose land and, indeed, a growing movement against it. It was realised that the more efficient management of existing commons was, in many cases, preferable to the expense of division and enclosure. The Commons Regulation Act passed in this year allowed unstinted commons to be stinted, with improved access and regulated rights of cutting peat. Under this legislation the commons of Crosby Garret, Winton, Kaber and Hartley (We), and the parts of east Stainmore not considered worth enclosing were regulated and managed more efficiently.

3. *Patterns of enclosure*

The enclosure of upland commons under parliamentary act started later and continued longer than the enclosure of open fields and lowland commons in the midlands and southern England, partly because enclosure gradually diffused out from a core area in a broad belt of country running from south-central to north-east England, and because the poorer quality of much of the land involved did not make it first choice for improvement.[4] In 1800 the north west region had the highest proportion of waste land of any English region. Between the late eighteenth and late nineteenth centuries in Westmorland over 100,000 acres (40,470ha), some 21 per cent of the area, was enclosed by parliamentary act. The figures for Cumberland were over 276,000 acres (111,697ha) (24 per cent) and for north Lancashire 50,000 acres (20,235ha) (22 per cent). It is impossible to calculate a precise figure for the total area enclosed as many awards did not give an accurate total surveyed area.[5] With such acts the area of allotments, quarries and public watering places can be totalled to give a fairly accurate figure but the amount of land occupied by new public and private roads is not always listed. The detailed patterns of parliamentary enclosure in Westmorland and north Lancashire are shown in Maps 3–6.

The origins of parliamentary enclosure in the north west lie in the early-mid eighteenth century, with evidence of increasing interest from the 1750s. It was often the customary tenants rather than the major landowners who took the lead in this. For example in 1752 some of the tenants of Dalston (Cu), south of Carlisle, petitioned the Bishop of Carlisle about having their common enclosed, though it was not until 1803 that an act was finally passed.[6] Efforts were made to enclose Cartmel (La) as early as 1768.[7] In Cumberland, seven acts relating to over 16,000 acres (6,475ha) of common pasture had been passed by 1770 and six awards completed. In Lancashire 13 acts covering over 5,500 acres (2,226ha), including some in the north of the county, had been passed and completed by 1770, including Ellel (La) on the fringes of Bowland for which an act had been passed as early as 1756. Westmorland, more remote, was a little slower to begin enclosure than Cumberland or Lancashire but even here the first enclosure acts had been passed by 1770. One influence encouraging the start of parliamentary enclosure is likely to have been enclosure agreements arranged privately without recourse to Parliament. As we have seen the amalgamation and enclosure of open field strips by private agreement was a long-established process in the region so that by the late eighteenth century there was very little land left in open field.[8] By the eighteenth century such agreements were also being used to divide and enclose areas of pasture. At least four instances are recorded in Westmorland before 1770. The earliest known so far, the

Map 3 (*opposite*): Parliamentary enclosure in north Westmorland. Map drawn by Chris Beacock.

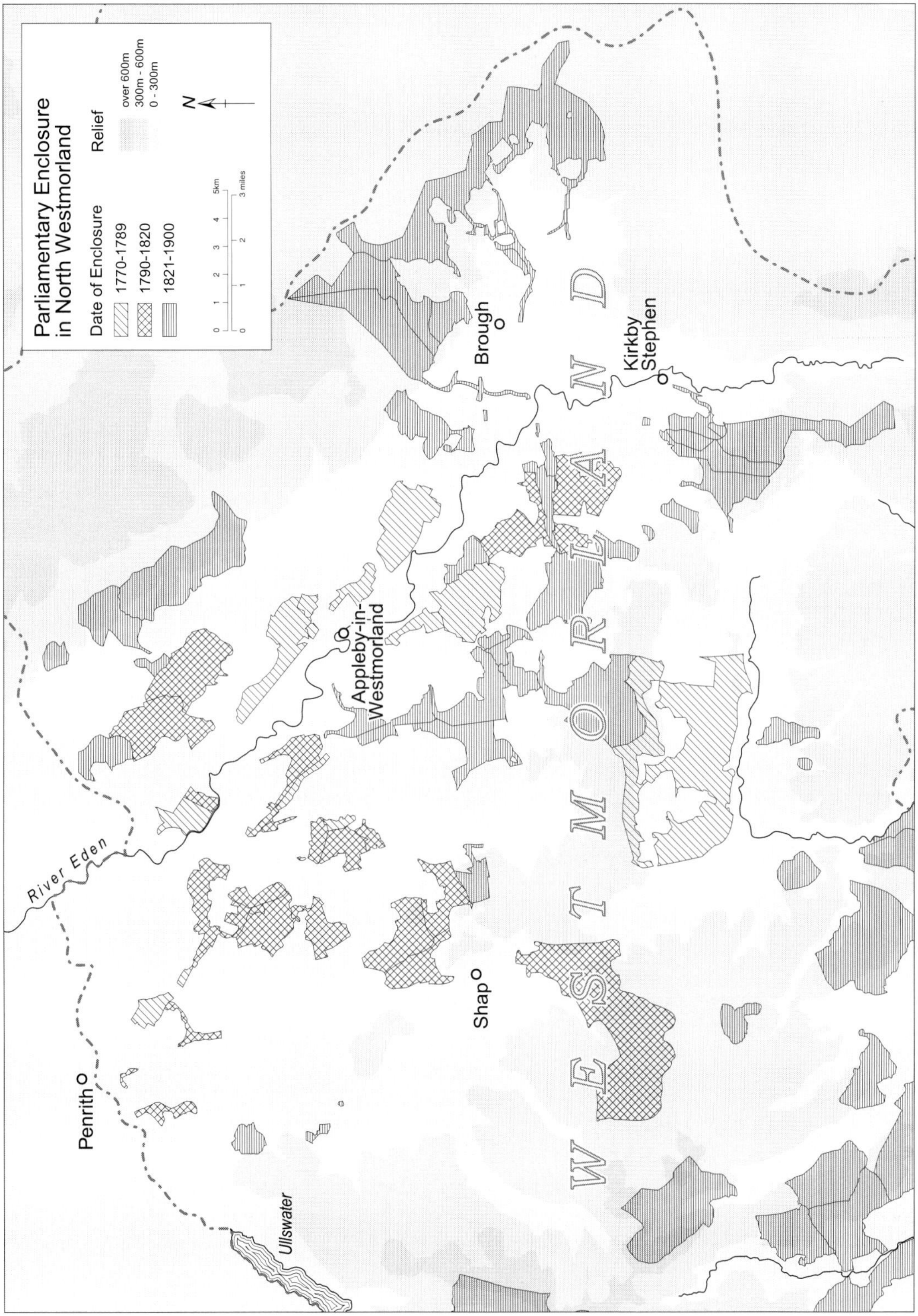
Parliamentary Enclosure
in North Westmorland
Date of Enclosure
1770-1789
1790-1820
1821-1900
Relief
over 600m
300m - 600m
0 - 300m
N
0 1 2 3 4 5km
0 1 2 3 miles
Brough
Kirkby Stephen
Appleby-in-Westmorland
Shap
Penrith
River Eden
Ullswater
WESTMORLAND

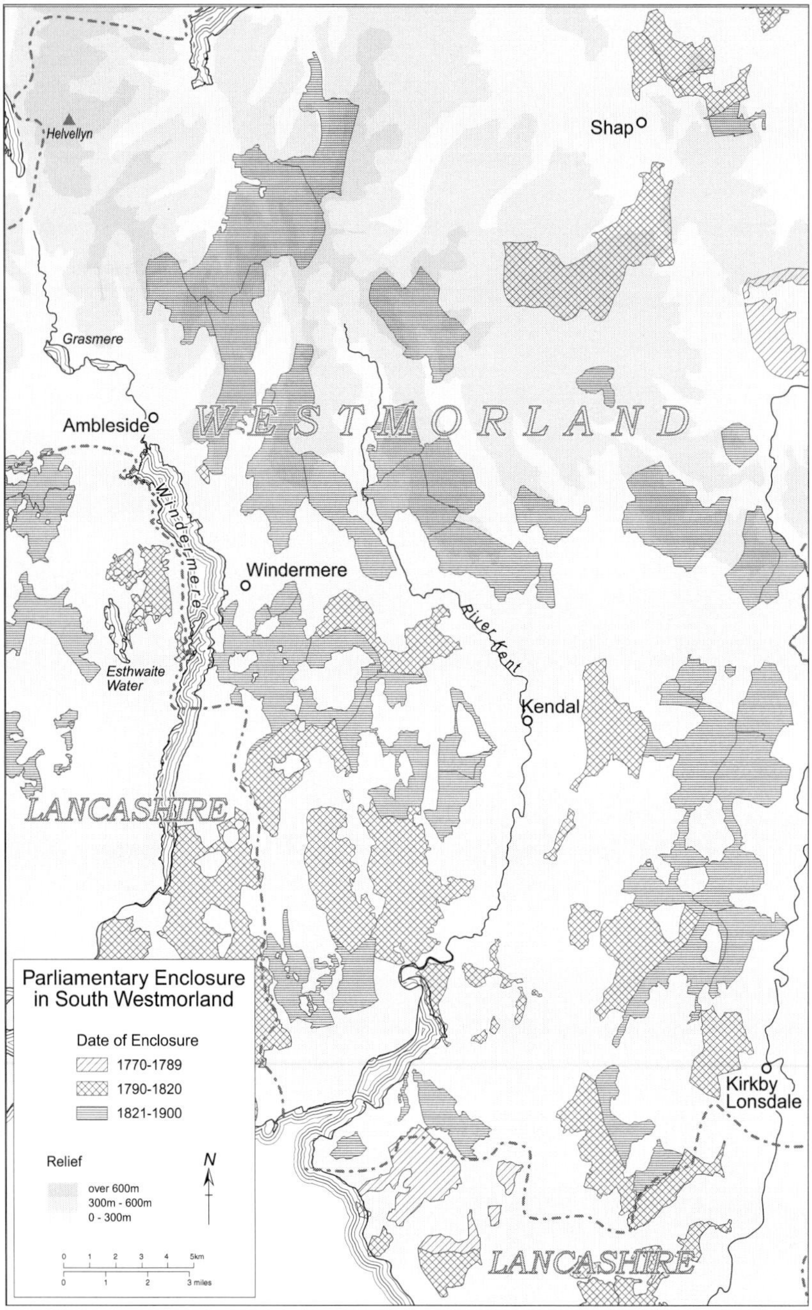

Map 4: Parliamentary enclosure in south Westmorland. Map drawn by Chris Beacock.

division of a 130-acre stinted pasture called Low Close in the township of Morland, occurred in 1756.[9] Although this enclosure process is recorded by only a brief and simple document, the task of surveying and dividing the land was undertaken by three local yeomen from other parishes in roles analogous to those of later parliamentary enclosure commissioners.

Map 5: Parliamentary enclosure in Furness and Cartmel. Map drawn by Chris Beacock.

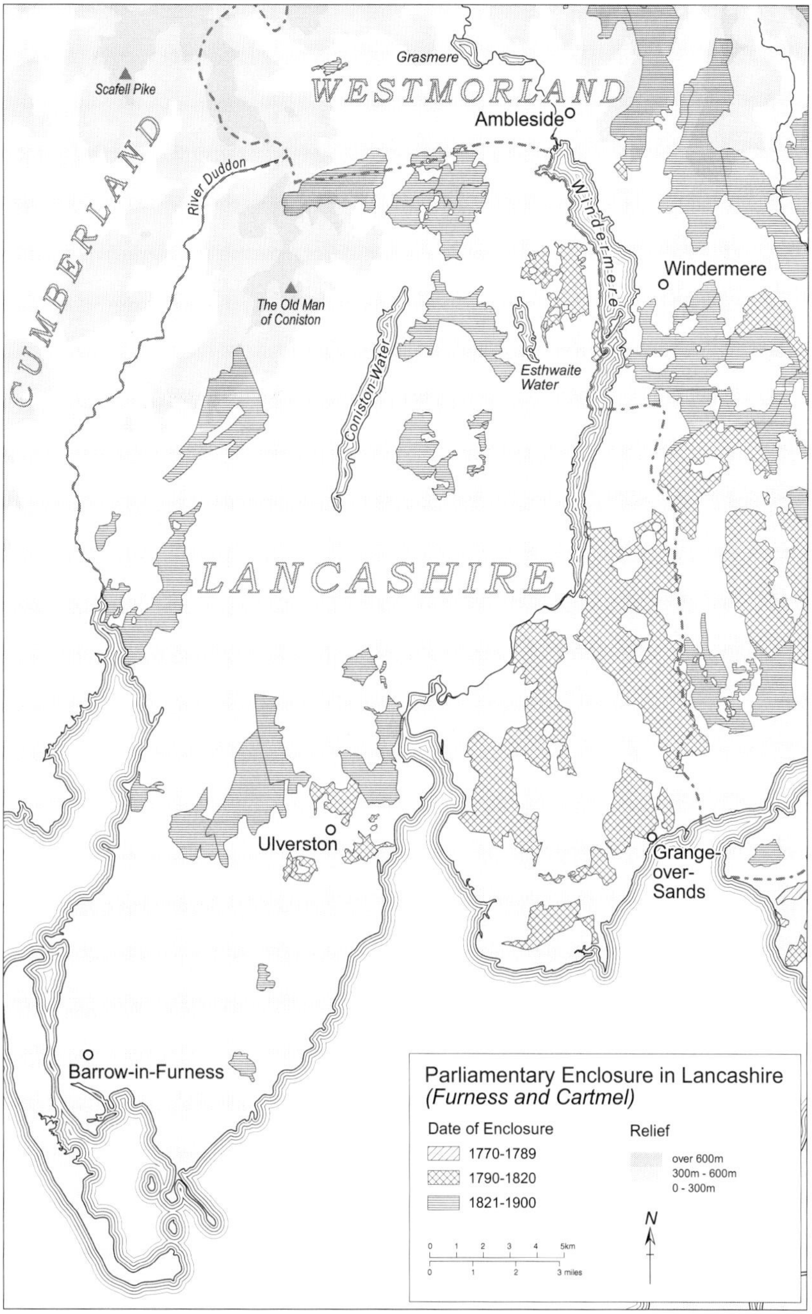

The privately-agreed enclosure in 1769 of the commons in the township of Crackenthorpe near Appleby may have provided the catalyst which precipitated an early burst of parliamentary enclosure in north Westmorland during the 1770s.[10] Although the lord of the manor of Crackenthorpe, Richard Machell, was not a major proprietor, his lands

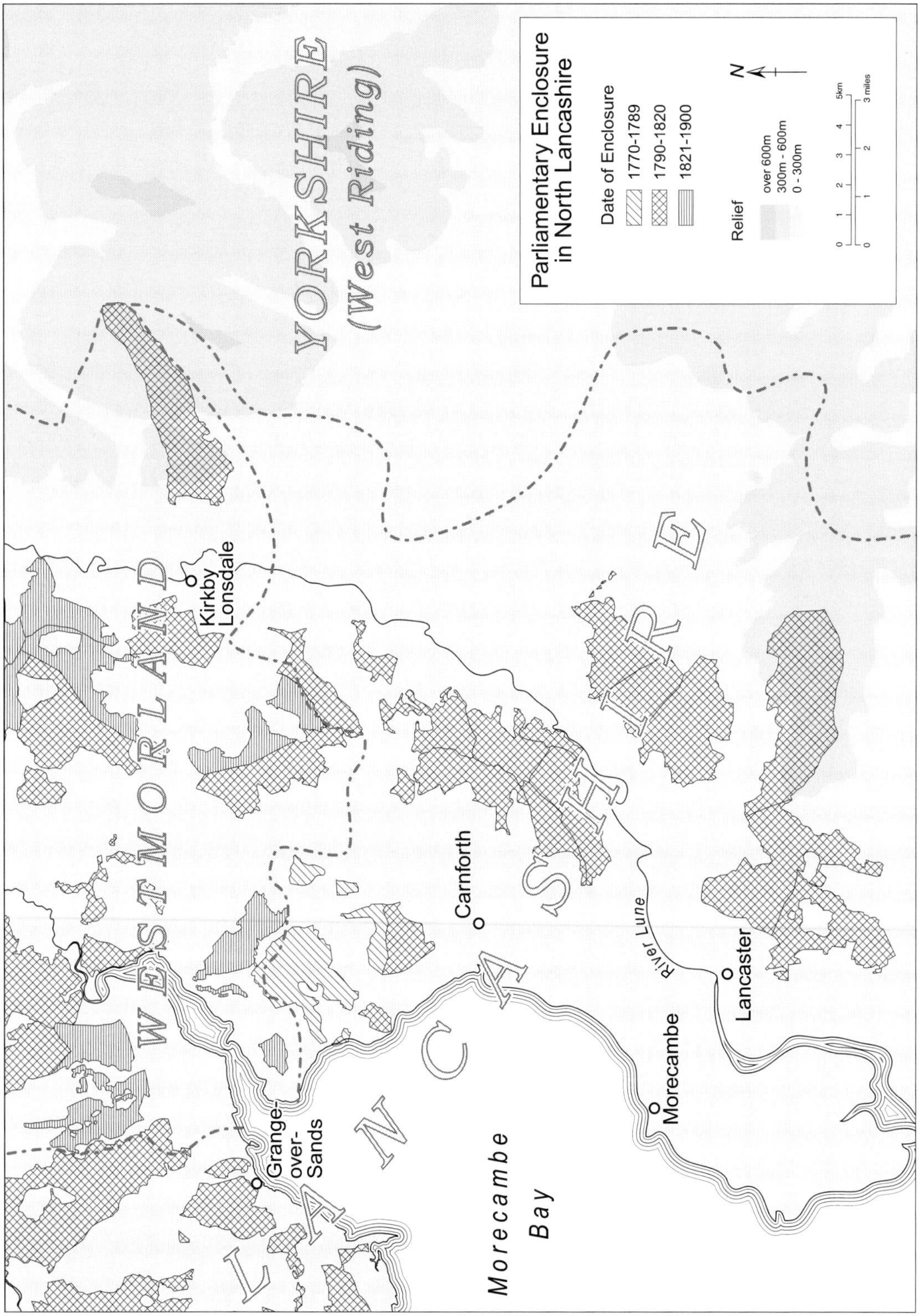
Parliamentary Enclosure
in North Lancashire
Date of Enclosure
1770-1789
1790-1820
1821-1900
Relief
over 600m
300m - 600m
0 - 300m
N
5km
3 miles
YORKSHIRE
(West Riding)
WESTMORLAND
LANCASHIRE
Kirkby Lonsdale
Carnforth
Grange-over-Sands
Morecambe
Lancaster
River Lune
Morecambe Bay

Map 6 (*opposite*): Parliamentary enclosure in north Lancashire. Map drawn by Chris Beacock.

adjoined the estates of the Earl of Thanet, an absentee landlord whose land agent in Appleby, Thomas Heelis, was one of the witnesses to the Crackenthorpe agreement. It is unlikely to be a coincidence that the first enclosure under parliamentary act to be completed in north Westmorland, the year after the Crackenthorpe enclosure, was for the adjoining manor of Brampton, or that Thomas Heelis was one of the commissioners.

Parliamentary enclosure in Cumbria and north Lancashire involved some 256 acts and was spread over more than a century from the late 1750s to the later nineteenth century. Table 1 shows the amount of enclosure accomplished in each decade. The dates relate to the completion of the enclosure awards rather than the passing of the acts as these reflected more accurately the date at which the bulk of the work of enclosure actually took place. Enclosure occurred in three main bursts: the first in the 1770s and the second during the Napoleonic Wars, paralleling trends further south. Unlike southern arable areas, however, there was also a third peak of activity in the mid nineteenth century.

The first parliamentary enclosure act in Westmorland, dating from 1767, was for 158 acres of land on Kendal Fell, immediately outside the borough of Kendal. Both the purpose and the procedures involved were unusual. The aim was to enclose the land, which belonged to the town, and rent it out to provide an income which would help to finance street improvements and poor relief in the borough. The enclosed land was

Table 1. Parliamentary enclosure in north west England by date of award.

	Cumberland		Westmorland		N. Lancs.		Total	
	Acres	%	Acres	%	Acres	%	Acres	%
1750s	0	0	0	0	1,991	4.0	1,991	0.5
1760s	15,124	5.5	158	0.2	0	0	15,282	3.6
1770s	10,160	3.8	9,618	9.5	1,210	2.4	20,988	4.9
1780s	12,340	4.9	0	0	0	0	12,340	2.9
1790s	4,326	1.6	723	0.7	1,500	3.0	6,549	1.5
1800s	22,980	8.3	1,536	1.5	19.741	39.5	44.257	10.3
1810s	86,887	31.3	14,515	14.4	9,068	18.1	110,469	25.8
1820s	50,866	18.4	25,375	25.2	5,650	11.3	81,891	19.1
1830s	14,552	5.3	4,524	4.5	807	1.6	19,883	4.7
1840s	16,173	5.9	10,629	10.5	3,226	6.4	30,028	7.0
1850s	7,754	2.7	20,788	20.6	3,256	6.5	31,798	7.4
1860s	18,553	6.7	6,435	6.4	3,676	7.2	28,664	6.7
1870s	11,171	3.9	2,157	2.1	0	0	13,323	3.1
1880s	5,300	1.9	641	0.6	0	0	5,941	1.4
1890s	500	0.2	4,075	4.0	0	0	4,575	1.1
Total	276,686		101,016		50,125		427,865	

(Source: Tate, 1978)

overseen by a board of twelve trustees, elected by the inhabitants of Kendal.[11] Two other more conventional enclosure acts, for Reagill and Shap, were also passed in 1767 but due to the deaths of the commissioners nothing was done and new acts to enclose the commons in these manors had to be passed in 1803 and 1813 respectively.[12] The earliest parliamentary enclosure in Westmorland to be completed for a substantial area, Orton, the act for which was passed in 1769, took ten years to accomplish and caused major problems because of the way in which it was handled (see below).

Overall, enclosure started slowly in the 1750s and 1760s, building up to a first, minor, peak in the 1770s with a marked drop in activity in the 1780s and 1790s. There was a sharp rise to a second, major peak in the first two decades of the nineteenth century when nearly 45 per cent of all enclosure was accomplished. Then there was a third, smaller, peak in the 1840s and 1850s with a slow tail off to the end of the century. Within this broad pattern, however, there were differences between the three counties. In Cumberland trends tended to begin and end sooner than in Westmorland, more distant from urban and industrial markets. North Lancashire had more of its enclosure concentrated in the first two decades of the nineteenth century – nearly 58 per cent – than other counties, with none after the 1860s. This may be due to the great potential of land in the relatively low country of Cartmel, Furness and the Lune valley for cultivation and the proximity of markets in the industrial areas in Furness and towns such as Kendal, Lancaster, and Ulverston. Cumberland had a less sharp third peak in the mid-nineteenth century – 8.6 per cent in the 1840s and 1850s – compared with Westmorland (30.7 per cent for the same two decades). This emphasises the importance of local-scale factors such as variations in the quality of transport networks and access to markets.

Patterns of landownership were also influential determinants of the timing of enclosure. Much of the late-eighteenth century burst of enclosure in Westmorland occurred in the Eden valley, particularly on lowland commons where the quality of the land was relatively high. Most of these commons were in manors belonging to the eighth Earl of Thanet who was actively building up his estates around Appleby Castle at this period.[13] Searle has suggested that the principal reason behind the enclosure of Cumbrian commons at this time was the damage which was being done to them by overstocking linked to the cattle droving trade, and the inability of manorial courts to regulate such abuses effectively.[14] However, there is strong evidence that around Appleby, the most important grain market in Westmorland at this time, the primary aim behind the enclosure of this relatively good land was the conversion of pasture to arable.[15] This is hinted at by provisions in the awards themselves. The ban on keeping sheep in the new enclosures for seven or even ten years to prevent damage to young hedges, a clause that featured in most of the 1770s acts from the Eden valley, was an incentive to use the land for arable, as was the stipulation, in awards like Great Ormside (1773) and Bongate and Burrells Moor (1774), that land within the new enclosures that was sown with cereals should pay only half tithes of grain for the first seven years.

Because tithes were not completely extinguished on some of the earliest enclosures their land use at the time of the tithe surveys in the 1830s and 1840s can be examined. Table 2 shows the high proportion of land under crop at this time on the enclosed lands of Brampton, Brougham and Temple Sowerby with lower, but still significant, figures in less well-drained Crackenthorpe and Sandford. Where enclosure had been undertaken on poorer soils at slightly higher altitudes, as in Bleatarn, Great Ormside and King's Meaburn where a belt of soil occurred which was described as being a 'cold ungrateful clay, very profitless to the farmer',[16] the percentage of arable was much lower. The proportion of land in cultivation in the cases mentioned above may well have fallen substantially from the early years of enclosure for Webster mentions Bleatarn and Great Ormside among the areas in which crop returns soon declined with much land being left to revert to pasture after 1815.[17]

Poor management and overcropping was a feature of at least some of this newly-improved land. Hutchinson, writing in 1794, described the enclosure of land in areas like Sowerby (Cu) some 26 years before. The new fields had borne luxuriant crops for a few years but soon became worn out with too much liming and too many cereal crops.[18] At Ellel (La) the land taken into cultivation after the award of 1756, despite being limed, had reverted to rough pasture after a few years over-intensive

Table 2. Use of enclosed land as recorded in tithe surveys of some north Westmorland townships.

	Date Enclosed	Date of Tithe	Arable %	Arable & pasture %	Arable & Meadow %
Bleatarn	1791	1846	34	16	
Brampton	1772	1841	76		7
Brougham	1776	1839	85		
Burrels	1776	1843	18		
Crackenthorpe	1769	1843	53		
Great Ormside	1773	1845	24	27	
King's Meaburn	1779	1841	13		
Sandford	1773	1844	52		
Temple Sowerby	1774	1840	96		

(Source: Tithe Surveys)

cropping with cereals and was only starting to recover again by the end of the century.[19]

In Cumberland nine acts were passed during the 1770s for commons in both the Eden valley and west Cumbria. Enclosure in north Lancashire in the 1770s was much more limited. The lack of enclosure in south Westmorland during the 1770s was probably due to the fact that there was much less waste on lower-lying good-quality land around Kendal than in the environs of Appleby. The drop in the amount of enclosure during the 1780s and 1790s has been attributed, at a national scale, to low grain prices and rising interest rates.[20]

The Kendal district, however, shared in the burst of enclosure during the Napoleonic Wars where a good deal of higher and poorer land was taken in with the aim of extending the arable area. Much of the straight, narrow ridge and furrow which can still be seen on such areas of former common was probably created at this time. As in the late eighteenth century the cultivation of newly-enclosed land was often too intensive. The 1801 crop returns for Morland, west of Appleby, stated that high grain prices had encouraged farmers to plough newly-enclosed land to a greater degree than was consistent with good husbandry.[21] However, high prices and political events were driving farmers to plough up marginal land. In this period of intense patriotism the improvement of the waste was seen as a way of helping to defeat the French. In 1803, Sir John Sinclair wrote that 'we have begun another campaign against the foreign enemies of the country...why should we not attempt a campaign against our domestic foe, I mean the hitherto unconquered sterility of so large a proportion of the surface of the kingdom'.[22] John Holt, who wrote the Board of Agriculture Report on Lancashire in 1795, commented 'Why seek out distant countries to cultivate when so much remains to be done at home?'.[23]

Not only was it more difficult and expensive to import grain during wartime: poor weather conditions and thin harvests also pushed up prices. Fourteen of the 22 harvests between 1793 and 1814 were deficient.[24] The war years of the early nineteenth century saw thousands of acres of land enclosed and ploughed up in the north west, a period of profit that Westmorland farmers remembered as the 'Bonneyparte (Bonaparte) Time'.[25] Around the head of Morecambe Bay a good deal of coastal wetland was also drained and enclosed, giving rise to some of the most regular enclosure landscapes in the region in the Lyth valley and the south coast of Cartmel. Extensive areas of common were also reclaimed on either side of the Lune above Lancaster and on the fringes of Bowland. In Cumberland 28,000 acres (11,332ha) of Inglewood Forest between Penrith and Carlisle was enclosed at this time as well as 20,000 acres (8,094ha) on Alston Moor.

There is little doubt that high grain prices were an important influence behind this burst of enclosure. A price series for wheat and oatmeal recorded in the *Lancaster Gazette* shows that prices had reached high levels before the Peace of Amiens in February 1802; wheat was 55 shillings and oatmeal 67s. 9d. per load of 4.5 Winchester bushels. Prices dropped to 50 and 24 shillings respectively during the peace but rose steadily with the return of wartime conditions to reach a peak of 103 shillings for wheat and 97s. 3d. for oatmeal during the autumn of 1812, described at the time as 'famine prices'. Thereafter they fell slowly until the end of 1813 with another peak, during which oatmeal reached 72 shillings per load, during 1817, a year which saw very poor harvests throughout Europe.[26] The impact of the intake of new land as a result of these pressures was significant. In July 1815 the *Lancaster Gazette* recorded that over 8,000 acres (3,238ha) of waste land had recently been brought into cultivation in Westmorland. The effect of this on the Kendal market has been 'striking'; the county had become a new exporter of grain where previously it had been a net importer.[27]

Enthusiasm for improvement in the early nineteenth century was tempered by an appreciation of the poor quality of much of the land involved. Some acts deliberately excluded areas of rough pasture which were so high lying that there would have been no profit, and much needless expense, in enclosing them. At Dufton (We), under the escarpment of Cross Fell, an extensive area was left out of the act for this reason. At Casterton (We) the highest parts of Casterton Fell were included within the act but with the proviso that allotments in this area did not have to be fenced and that the boundaries of the former common only needed to be established and marked. At Hutton Roof (We) the extensive pastures on areas of limestone pavement were left unenclosed and simply converted from an unregulated common to a stinted pasture (Figure 5). At Broughton in Furness (La), Broughton High Moor was to be left unenclosed if the proprietors wished it (Figure 6).[28] A draft map for the Preston Patrick enclosure (We), drawn about 1814, marks the higher-lying allotments as 'unploughable', probably due as much to poor drainage as to altitude.[29] In Caton (La) the poor peaty moors of Blanch Fell and Black Fell, covering Clougha Pike, were simply appointed to be divided into cattlegates.

After Waterloo and the return of peace in 1815 agricultural prices fell sharply, causing a slump. A farm at Sedbergh which had been rented for £85 in 1815 went for only £23 10s. the following year. In 1817 at Kendal hiring fair, young men who would have been hired as farm workers for £20 to £30 a few years before were happy to get places for £10 to £13.[30] At Broughton in Furness tenant farmers were absconding leaving arrears of rent unpaid.[31] Not surprisingly the rate of enclosure slowed markedly. The third burst of enclosure, from the 1820s to the mid-nineteenth century, was linked almost entirely with the improvement of pasture,

Figure 5: Hutton Roof Crags was left unenclosed as a stinted sheep pasture because it was clearly unsuited to improvement.

Figure 6: Allotments on the higher parts of the Preston Patrick enclosure were considered 'unploughable'.

mainly for sheep farming, encouraged both by the General Enclosure Act of 1845 which speeded up the process and reduced costs, and the spread of the railway network which provided much faster access for livestock and their products to the markets of industrial south Lancashire, Yorkshire, Tyneside and even London (Figure 7).[32] In Cumberland only 5.3 per cent of the county was enclosed after 1830 but in Westmorland 8.8 per cent, showing a time lag due, perhaps, to poorer access to markets before the coming of the railways.[33] Considerable capital was sometimes invested in improving such land. On the large allotment received by the Earl of Lonsdale on Shap Fells with the award of 1820 over 1,200 acres

Figure 7: A bridge on the former railway line over Stainmore, opened in 1862. Railways like this encouraged land improvement in the north west.

(486ha) was improved by liming and c.1,500 (607ha) acres by tile draining, converting it from rough grazing into improved pasture.[34]

There were marked contrasts in the history of enclosure at a local level. The enclosure of Orton (We), for example, was begun in 1769 while the award for the manor of Asby Winderwath (We), on the other side of the watershed, was not made until 1874, and the parish of Crosby Ravensworth (We), adjoining them both, was never enclosed at all. The differences in subsequent land improvement and grazing management between high-quality grassland on the Orton side of the boundary and heather moorland on the Crosby Ravensworth side is striking today (Figure 8). At this scale differences in patterns of land ownership and social structure could produce very different decisions regarding whether or not to enclose, but it is difficult to identify the reasons behind such contrasts.

Not all enclosure during the late eighteenth and nineteenth centuries was conducted under the aegis of a parliamentary act. When the number of landholders with rights over an area of common, or particularly a stinted pasture, was small and there was no opposition to division it was still possible, and much cheaper, to enclose by unanimous agreement without reference to Parliament, using privately-appointed commissioners. Areas of privately-arranged enclosure can often be identified on the map from the regular field boundaries lying outside known areas of parliamentary enclosure. Documentation for such enclosure is more

Figure 8: The contrast between improved pasture on the enclosed lands of Orton (left) and heather moorland on the unimproved common of Crosby Ravensworth (right) is striking.

elusive than for parliamentary enclosure. Even though agreements were often modelled on parliamentary procedures there was no requirement for copies of them to be deposited with local justices. They may survive among estate collections or parish papers. In Westmorland 14 private enclosures have been identified. A number of cases are also known from north Lancashire including one of 771 acres (312ha) in Satterthwaite.

It is not so much necessary to explain why enclosure by private agreement survived as why parliamentary enclosure became so dominant. Enclosure by private agreement tended to be favoured for fairly limited areas between small groups of landowners, circumstances in which unanimous agreement over the desirability of dividing and enclosing the land was more likely to be achieved. Parliamentary enclosure was more useful where there was opposition to enclosure, or at least apathy, on the part of at least some landowners but it was a much more expensive process. Privately-agreed enclosures often involved the same general procedures. Thus the enclosure of Thwaite Head and Bruntwood Fell in Rusland (La) in 1842 was overseen by two commissioners with full powers to hear all claims and to examine the evidence of witnesses under oath if necessary in order to determine rights and boundaries. A surveyor was employed to produce a map and a public award was to be made. The area concerned was only just over 151 acres (61ha).[35] But by operating privately corners could be cut and costs trimmed. In 1861, Charles

Dickson Archibald of Rusland Hall and a few other proprietors agreed to the division of Souterholme Meadows at Rusland. They appointed Crayston Webster, the Kendal land surveyor who had been active in many parliamentary enclosure proceedings. But they added a proviso to the agreement that, if he considered that any existing maps of the area were sufficiently accurate, a new survey could be dispensed with.[36]

Notes

1. R.A. Jarvis, et al., *Soils and their uses in Northern England*, Soil Survey of England and Wales Bulletin 10, pp.145, 305; W. Hutchinson, *The History of the County of Cumberland and some Places Adjacent* (Jollie, 1794), vol 1, p.345.
2. Select Committee on Commons Inclosure, 1844, Command Paper 583, vol 5.
3. W.E. Tate (ed), *A Domesday of English Enclosure Awards* (University of Reading, 1978).
4. A. B. Humphries, 'Agrarian Change in East Cumberland, 1750–1900', Unpublished M.Phil.Thesis, University of Lancaster, 1993, pp.135–9; M.E. Turner, *English Parliamentary Enclosure* (Dawson, 1980), p.34.
5. J. Chapman & T. Harris, 'The accuracy of enclosure estimates: some evidence from Northern England', *Journal of Historical Geography* 8 (3) (1982), pp.261–64.
6. Humphries, Agrarian Change, pp.188–9.
7. J. Stockdale, *Annals of Cartmel* (Kitchin, 1872), p.327.
8. G. Elliot, 'Field systems of North West England', in A.R.H. Baker, & R.A.Butlin eds., *Studies of Field Systems in the British Isles* (Cambridge University Press, 1973), pp.41–92.
9. CRO (Kendal) WPM/5.
10. CRO (Kendal) WD/HH/15.
11. CRO (Kendal) WSMB/K, Kendal Fell Trust Minute Book 1767–1793.
12. Tate, *Domesday of Enclosure*, pp.264–265.
13. C.E. Searle, '"The Odd Corner of England": a study of a rural social formation in transition, Cumbria c.1700–c1914', Unpublished PhD. Thesis, University of Essex, 1984, pp.195–200.
14. C.E. Searle, 'Customary tenants and the enclosure of the Cumbrian commons', *Northern History* 29 (1993), pp.126–53.
15. Statistical Account of the Parish of Orton. *Monthly Magazine* No 98 (1803) CRO (Kendal)WDY 269.
16. C. Webster, 'The farming of Westmorland', *Journal of the Royal Society of Agriculture of England* 2nd ser. 4 (1868), pp.6–7.
17. *Ibid.*
18. Hutchinson, *History of Cumberland*, p.519.
19. J. Holt, *General View of the Agriculture of the County of Lancaster* (Nicol, 1795), p.48.
20. G.E. Mingay, *Parliamentary Enclosure in England: an introduction to its causes, incidence, and impact, 1750–1850* (Longman, 1998), p.22.
21. M. Turner (ed), *The 1801 crop returns for England* (Institute of Historical Research, 1978), 5/48 Morland.
22. E. Halevy, *A History of the English People in the Nineteenth Century Vol I : England in 1815* (Benn, 1949), p.230.

23. Holt, *General View*, p.86.
24. J.V. Beckett, *The Agricultural Revolution* (Blackwell, 1990), p.65.
25. Webster, Farming of Westmorland, p.7.
26. Anonymous, *Lancaster records, or leaves from local history, 1801–1850* (G.C. Clark, 1869); J.D. Post, *The Last Great Subsistence Crisis in the Western World* (John Hopkins, 1977).
27. Anonymous, *Lancaster Records*, p.81.
28. CRO (Barrow) BD 17.
29. CRO (Kendal) WD/RIG 1244.
30. Anonymous, *Local Chronicle* (Kendal, 1865).
31. CRO (Barrow) BD 17/4–5.
32. M.E. Shepherd, 'The small owner in Cumbria c.1840–1910: a case study from the upper Eden valley', *Northern History* 35 (1999), pp.163, 168.
33. Searle, Customary tenants, p.291.
34. Webster, Farming of Westmorland, pp.35–36.
35. LRO DDAr.238.
36. LRO DDAr.246.

CHAPTER FOUR

Enclosure: for and against

1. *The advantages of enclosure*

The reasons behind parliamentary enclosure in England generally have been suggested as including changing the structure of rural society, increasing the profits from agriculture and providing social stability.[1] To what extent the major landowners of north west England had a broad agenda, including such social engineering in mind is not clear, but there were a number of quite specific advantages behind enclosure. Obtaining an act of parliament provided legal certification of the process which could not easily be challenged. It also, incidentally, provided a formal mechanism for opposition to enclosure to be heard. More specifically, the advantages of the enclosure of upland waste and commons in this area, as already mentioned, have been seen principally as the removal of the problem of deterioration of commons by over-grazing, especially through the agistment of livestock from outside the community.[2] A good deal of this pressure was generated by the cattle droving trade. Animals from Scotland were grazed en route to their markets further south. In addition, local graziers bought lean Scottish animals and fattened them up on their pastures. The removal of peat and turf from commons was also damaging. At Bolton (We) in the early nineteenth century it was agreed that, as a result of this, if the common was not enclosed soon it would be ruined.[3] But, as has been shown, particularly during the 1770s and the Napoleonic Wars, enclosure also allowed the conversion of suitable, and sometimes less suitable, pasture land to arable. Other advantages included the ability to improve pasture in individual ownership by liming and to raise the quality of livestock by selective breeding.

Another potential use for enclosed land was afforestation. This was undertaken on a large scale in parts of the Lake District, notably by John Christian Curwen at Claife on the west side of Windermere and by the Bishop of Llandaff at Gummers How at the south end of the lake.[4] Where the quality of the soil was relatively low but the degree of exposure moderate a significant proportion of the land on some awards was planted, especially in the low undulating country east of Windermere. Large moorland allotments could be also turned into grouse moor.[5] An additional advantage for those with rights on commons which adjoined the settlements of Bowness and Windermere was that enclosure allowed plots of land to be sold off for the construction of villas and mansions for well-to-do incomers. The higher ground above the east side of Windermere, which was enclosed in 1822, provided a number of ideal viewpoints for such houses.[6] A desire to develop land for housing on the outskirts of Lancaster may have been a motive behind the enclosure of Caton and Scotforth commons (Figure 9).

Enclosure ended the depletion of the resources of commons by unauthorised encroachments, a widespread problem on Cumbrian commons.[7] Enclosure may also have reduced the theft of sheep: it certainly stopped the widespread practice of 'dogging', where farmers used dogs to drive off neighbours' sheep from the best parts of commons to make way for their own. This was mentioned by Webster[8] as being a widespread abuse in Westmorland and is supported by cases such as one from Sleagill in 1802 which went to the Quarter Sessions in Appleby where Matthew Ewbank drove off 200 sheep and 200 lambs belonging to George Shaw so that 50 animals were lost and 50 killed, the remainder taking a lot of time and trouble to round up.[9] At Casterton dogging was done particularly by the larger farmers who were attempting to monopolise the common.[10] On the adjoining Leck Fell one or two men living nearest the common succeeded in denying rightful access to other commoners. This was stated to be the main reason behind seeking an enclosure act.[11] The problem of dogging seemed to be especially bad on

Figure 9: 'Moorlands': A mansion built on an enclosure allotment on the former Caton Moor.

the extensive commons surrounding Dent, Garsdale and Sedbergh (Yo). Evidence submitted to the Select Committee on Commons Inclosure in 1844 mentioned some striking examples, such as the case of Mr Edmond Bannister of Cowgill, Dent, whose flock of about 100 sheep had recently been driven off the common by a neighbour's dogs and which were found scattered over Mallerstang, Kirkby Stephen and Ravenstonedale on the far side of the Howgills. What was virtually internecine warfare in Dent in the early 1840s included not only the dogging and slaughter of sheep but the maiming and killing of horses and fights between shepherds.[12] Overstocking was also rife with people from outside Dent leasing a couple of acres of land and then putting 700 or 800 sheep on the common.[13] Even worse were situations where people who did not even have common rights excluded those who did. At Natland (We) also in the early 1840s, the grazings on the Helm were denied to the commoners by four or five families of itinerant potters who settled there during the winter months and drove off all other livestock, 'a most unmanageable set of beings' as a witness described them.[14]

Enclosure also removed other problems relating to commons such as boundary disputes, disagreements over intercommoning between townships, arguments over who had common rights, and the straying back to their original pastures of hefted sheep which had been sold to other local farms.[15]

Another benefit of enclosure was the improvement of transport by turning frequently-impassable local tracks into good all-weather roads using Macadam's technique of pounding small stones together until they interlocked, creating an all-weather surface. The public and private roads laid out by surveyors of highways acting for the enclosure commissioners facilitated the import of lime for agricultural improvement and the marketing of produce, as well as making communications between neighbouring communities faster and easier. At a local level they had as great an impact as the turnpikes at a regional scale.[16] The drainage of marshes and mosses which was associated with enclosure may even have had beneficial effects on the health of local inhabitants. In Cartmel people believed that enclosure had banished 'ague', possibly malaria, from the parish.[17]

2. *Opposition to enclosure*

The advantages of enclosure might seem clear today but this was not necessarily so at the time. Several attempts were sometimes made before an enclosure act was eventually passed by Parliament. In the case of Broughton in Furness an early attempt at enclosure, with the intention of applying to Parliament, was made in 1771. The reasons for its failure are not clear but a second attempt in 1815 was almost certainly the victim of unfortunate timing, coinciding with the post-Napoleonic Wars slump. An act was only passed in 1828 and even then the award was not completed until 1847.[18]

Who were the promoters of enclosure and how much opposition did they experience? In the case of open-field arable and lowland commons in the midlands and the south of England there is a general presumption that enclosure was often favoured by the larger landowners, and was detrimental to small farmers, cottagers and squatters who, in some cases, opposed enclosure but mostly unsuccessfully. There is indeed evidence that these groups did often suffer as a result of enclosure and that numbers of smaller cultivators were reduced through their selling their land to larger landowners because of their inability to afford the costs of enclosure.[19] In the north west things were generally different, due to the nature of the economy, the structure of rural society and the character of tenure. Instances occur where a single, dominant landowner may have forced enclosure through. At Claughton (La) the lord of the manor, Thomas Fenwick, received 638 acres (258ha) out of the total area of the common of 867 acres (351ha) and was clearly in a commanding position. But often, as will be discussed below, it was the ordinary customary tenants who pressed their manorial lords for enclosure.

Because most of the land was being enclosed from common pastures and was thus used more intensively after enclosure, in some cases being converted to arable, the amount of labour needed on the land would have tended to increase, even after the initial burst of demand for labour to create the new enclosure landscape, unlike parts of the midlands where, on enclosure, open field arable was laid down to grass, so that the amount of labour required fell. Another important factor in Cumbria was the survival of customary tenures derived from medieval Border tenure under which, in return for being required, when needed, to turn out and fight the Scots, tenants received security on their lands which amounted almost to freehold. These rights had survived even after the seventeenth century when the Scots ceased to raid across the Border. Under these customary tenures, still prevalent in the eighteenth century, tenants paid entry fines to the lord of their manor when either the lordship or tenancy changed hands. Such sources of income, which varied from manor to manor, could not be easily raised and tended to occur haphazardly so that for a manorial lord investment in their estate which required forward planning based on expected income was difficult. Because of their protected status, under which customary tenants had the right to pass land on to their heirs, landlords could not take land under their own direct management as was possible with ordinary leasehold when leases fell vacant. One way in which manorial lords could increase their income was by the enclosure of commons which allowed their shares to be converted into leasehold farms. Customary tenants were treated as landowners and received allotments, unlike leasehold tenants further south. In the process of enclosure Cumbrian customary tenants were generally enfranchised with their tenures being converted to freehold. So both landlords and customary tenants had motives for promoting enclosure and were generally in agreement regarding its desirability.[20] It has also been suggested that in Cumbria there was general accord between major landowners, gentry and farmers over the desirability of enclosure as a result of the deterioration of the commons through overgrazing.[21] The practice of selling a proportion of a common to pay for the expenses of the enclosure, which occurred in about half the awards in this region, also made enclosure less of a financial burden for smaller freeholders and customary tenants. Where opposition did occur it was usually due to local, specific issues rather than over the general desirability of enclosure.

There are a number of instances where it was the customary tenants rather than the major landowners who took the initiative over enclosure. At Preston Patrick (We) the majority of the tenants had written to the Earl of Lonsdale desiring an enclosure act.[22] At Reagill (We) it was considered vital that everybody 'let his property be ever so small' should be consulted about the desirability of enclosure.[23] Even so, some opposition did occur. A majority of three-quarters or, preferably, four-fifths, by value of property rather than numbers, was usually required for a bill to be accepted but a search of the House of Commons records indicates that a number of enclosure bills from the north west were dropped, some at least due to opposition, while in a smaller number of cases counter petitions were presented (Table 3). However, there are indications that counter petitions were often from individuals rather than groups, from people who were not opposed to enclosure as such but were concerned that the specific terms of a particular bill were detrimental to their rights.[24]

A notable case of large-scale opposition to enclosure was in the parish of Ravenstonedale (We) in 1767 when 91 people, customary tenants and small freeholders, signed a petition opposing an attempt by Sir James Lowther, the lord of the manor, to enclose the commons.[25] The petition was successful and the commons remain unenclosed today, despite a

Table 3. Opposition to north west enclosure acts.

	Bills submitted	Acts passed	Bills dropped	Counter petitions
Cumberland	119	81	38	13
Westmorland	86	47	39	5
Lancashire	99	66	33	11

(Source: Turner & Wray, 1991)

second attempt at enclosure in the later nineteenth century.[26] Elsewhere opposition was clearly only from a small minority. At Cliburn (We) in 1803, 24 landowners were in favour of the bill, seven against. The average rental valuation of the property in the township of those supporting enclosure was £7 10s. 3d. and for those against only £4 16s. 1d. indicating that opposition came mainly from smaller landowners.[27] At Reagill in 1802, 17 landowners were for the bill, two against and three were deemed incapable (one was in the West Indies, one 'an idiot' and a third simply could not be traced) but here one of the opponents was a more substantial landowner who was against the bill as being 'contrary to the interest' of the township.[28] At Dufton in 1822 out of 49 owners none were against enclosure and only four were neutral.[29] At Yanwath near Penrith in 1812 the Quaker Thomas Wilkinson produced an anti-enclosure pamphlet arguing that the 150 acres (61ha) common of Yanwath Moor was not worth the expense of enclosing, and that the cottagers and smaller tenants would suffer as a result, but he was not supported by the rest of the customary tenants.[30]

Some opposition was more effective. At Asby in 1806–7 those opposed to the bill to enclose the commons of Asby Coatsworth manor – at least 13 of them – mounted a campaign in London to persuade absentee landowners in the capital to sign a petition opposing the bill which was presented to the House of Commons in 20 April 1807 by the MP, Colonel Lowther. For whatever reason the bill was dropped. Another bill to the same effect was presented to Parliament in 1813. Notwithstanding that the lord of the manor agreed to accept only a fortieth share of the land to facilitate the process no enclosure act was passed for this manor until 1845 though the reasons for the opposition are not clear.[31] In 1824 William Wordsworth successfully spoke out in defence of the rights of the statesmen farmers and against the proposals of agents of Lady de Fleming who planned to enclose the Rydal commons.[32]

That opposition was not simply a straightforward case of saying 'no' to the signing of a bill is shown by the example of the Broughton in Furness (La) enclosure. A document, undated but probably from around 1827–28, lists people with common rights and their position regarding the potential enclosure of the extensive commons, and the value of their property as measured by the land tax. People paying £19 8s. 3d. worth of land tax were broadly in favour of enclosure and those paying £4 13s. 4d. were against but within these general categories were many shades of opinion. On the side supporting enclosure some had signed the bill. There were also those who had not signed but declared that they did not object to the bill and would not oppose it, and those who were broadly in favour but believed that it would be better for only part of the common to be enclosed and the rest to be used as stinted pasture. Among the opposition were those who would not sign the bill at the moment but said that they would go with the majority of their neighbours if they decided to sign, those who would not sign but who believed that the common would be better divided than not, those who would not sign because they disapproved of the proposed commissioner, those who were scared of losing their rights to cut peat and turf and those with no specific objection but who might change their minds not to sign if there was a threat of the common being sold off.[33]

Although opposition to enclosure was not widespread in the north west the process sometimes brought to a head long-standing disputes between communities, particularly over boundaries between adjoining commons. In some cases such disputes were lengthy and complex, causing a significant delay in the implementation of enclosure. In a significant proportion of cases, particularly during the Napoleonic Wars, the completion of enclosure awards was delayed for reasons which are not always clear but which may have included a lack of experience on the part of commissioners. Disputes over boundaries, disagreements over claims and delays due to the deaths of commissioners can sometimes be discerned from the awards and particularly from other enclosure papers, but these only survive for a few enclosure processes

3. *Problems with enclosure: the case of Cartmel*

We know more about the background to the Cartmel enclosure, the act for which was passed in 1796, due to the survival of a variety of sources including a history of Cartmel written by James Stockdale, the son of one of the prime movers behind enclosure, a bundle of letters and other documents in the Cavendish of Holker papers, and a pro-enclosure pamphlet written by a member of the committee of proprietors which was appointed to draft the enclosure bill.

It is clear from the pamphlet that moves to enclose the commons were underway before August 1793, when a committee of 14 proprietors, two from each of the seven townships in the parish, was formed to draw up a bill which was to go to Parliament in 1794. This failed to happen. The reason, according to the pamphlet, was a groundswell of opposition. The anonymous writer dismissed as ridiculous fears that the Church, as owners of the tithes, and the enclosure commissioners would end up with most of the land. If such ideas were genuinely held it indicates that in this area there was a widespread lack of knowledge concerning the nature of the enclosure process. The author considered opposition from a few people who were profiting by abusing the existing common (presumably by overstocking) as something to be expected. Concerns over the rights of small proprietors and cottagers were dismissed by reference to an unspecified national authority who claimed that enclosure benefited rather than harmed smallholders. The defence was vague and woolly, perhaps deliberately, but it also seems likely that the inexperience of those who formed the committee may have had something to do with it. At this stage they still did not have a clear idea of the extent of the commons or even whether their area was similar to, or greater than, that of the enclosed land within the parish.[34]

References to an opposition group continue to surface in correspondence from 1794 and 1795 making it clear that a second attempt to get a bill through Parliament had failed. A letter to Lord Frederick Cavendish dated 30 April 1794 refers to a meeting concerning enclosure at which none of the opposition party were present.[35] In February 1795 one of Lord Cavendish's legal advisors wrote that even after counting on the support of Cavendish himself and the Bishop of Chester 'we shall have some difficulty in producing a majority in number and value'.[36] Cavendish seems to have been getting paranoid by this time because in a letter from him to the committee he referred to a suggestion produced by them, relating to the wording of one of the clauses in the draft bill, writing that such a suggestion 'could only have come from the most unacceptable want of imagination unless it should be a trick to defeat the bill.'[37]

That the opposition had good grounds for their concern is indicated by a letter from a member of the committee to Cavendish in which he forwards the suggestion of Mr. John Wilkinson of Castlehead that to save the cost of a survey the bulk of the commons, after deducting the tithe allotment, should be sold off in small lots to raise money, a plan which another landowner described as 'fraught with cruelty and injustice', favouring the wealthy and being detrimental to the smallholders.[38]

Clearly there was a lot going on behind the scenes here but while Wilkinson's scheme was rejected there is evidence (see Chapter 7) that the bill that was eventually accepted by Parliament was indeed detrimental to the poorer cottagers in the district.

Notes

1. R.C. Russell, 'Parliamentary Enclosure, Common Rights and Social Change: Evidence from the Parts of Lindsey in Lincolnshire', *Journal of Peasant Studies* 27 (4) (2000), pp.54–111.
2. C.E. Searle, 'Customary tenants and the enclosure of the Cumbrian commons', *Northern History* 29 (1993), pp.126–53.
3. CRO (Kendal) WQ/R/I Bolton misc. enclosure papers.
4. W.H. Pearsall, & W. Pennington, *The Lake District. A Landscape History* (Collins, 1973), p.294.
5. A. Done & R. Muir, 'The landscape history of grouse shooting in the Yorkshire Dales', *Rural History* 12 (2000), pp.195–210.
6. M. Andrews, *The Search for the Picturesque: landscape aesthetics and tourism in Britain 1760–1800* (Scolar, 1989), p.174.

7. J. Stockdale, *Annals of Cartmel* (Kitchin 1872), p.197.
8. C. Webster, 'On the Farming of Westmorland', *Journal of the Royal Agricultural Society of England* 2nd ser. Vol. 4 (1868), p.14.
9. CRO (Kendal) WQ/R/I Sleagill misc. enclosure papers.
10. C.E. Searle, '"The Odd Corner of England": a study of a rural social formation in transition, Cumbria c1700–c1914', Unpublished PhD. Thesis, University of Essex, 1984, p.166.
11. Select Committee on Commons Inclosure 1844 (Command paper 583) vol 5, p.124.
12. *Ibid.*, p.132.
13. *Ibid.*, p.127.
14. *Ibid.*
15. CRO (Kendal) WPR9/Z 13.
16. B.P. Hindle, *Roads and Trackways of the Lake District* (Moorland, 1984), pp.164, 172.
17. Stockdale, *Annals of Cartmel*, pp.327–8.
18. CRO (Barrow) BD 17 1–20.
19. K.D.M. Snell, *Annals of the Labouring Poor: social change and agrarian England, 1660–1900* (Cambridge University Press, 1985), pp.138–223.
20. Searle, Cumbrian customary tenants.
21. *Ibid.*
22. CRO (Kendal) WPR/47.
23. CRO (Kendal) WQ/R/I Reagill misc. enclosure papers.
24. M. Turner & T. Wray, 'A survey of sources for parliamentary enclosure: the House of Commons Journal and commissioners' working papers', *Archives* 19 (1991), pp.257–88.
25. CRO (Kendal) WDX/76.
26. CRO (Kendal) WDX/370/Z/2.
27. CRO (Kendal) WQ/R/I Cliburn misc. enclosure papers.
28. CRO (Kendal) WQ/R/I Reagill misc. enclosure papers.
29. C.E. Searle, 'Cumbria's parliamentary enclosure movement: a comparative case study in rural quiescence', *TCWAAS* Series 2, 95 (1995), p.249.
30. T. Wilkinson, *Thoughts on Inclosing Yanwath Moor and Round Table Addressed to the Claimants Theoron,* Armitt Library, (1812) .
31. CRO (Kendal) WQ/R/I Asby misc. enclosure papers.
32. J.R.V. Barker, *Wordsworth: a life* (Penguin, 2001), p.389.
33. CRO (Barrow) BD/17/8.
34. CRO (Barrow) BDX 84.
35. LRO DDCa 22/14/5.
36. LRO DDCa 22/14/24.
37. LRO DDCa 27/14/9.
38. LRO DDCa 27/14/2, 27/14/13.

CHAPTER FIVE

How enclosure was undertaken

1. *The commissioners and their work*

The earliest phases of enclosure involved discussions between local proprietors regarding the desirability, or otherwise, of enclosing local common lands. A lot of bargaining must often have taken place at this stage which is only recorded occasionally where correspondence survives. In particular, when tithes had not been commuted, as was quite often the case in the late eighteenth and early nineteenth centuries but rarely later on, after the Tithe Commutation Act of 1836, there were often protracted negotiations with the bishop over the church's share of the common given in return for extinguishing the right to collect tithes. At Cartmel, as we have seen, a committee of landowners was formed to draft a bill, not including the lord of the manor but closely in touch with him. Before the 1801 act introduced a set of acceptable standard clauses, there must have been much perusal of recent enclosure acts. In the case of the Cartmel committee acts passed in 1788 and 1789 relating to enclosures in Nottinghamshire, Northamptonshire and near Southampton were consulted.[1] There was considerable debate about the wording of each individual clause.

One of the first things that was done when planning to enclose a common was to approach local men with some standing but who did not have any direct interest in the lands of the parish, manor or township concerned, to see whether they would be prepared to act as commissioners. Before the 1770s large numbers of commissioners were sometimes appointed; for Ellel (La) there were no less than 17 of them. In 1767 six were appointed for Skelton (Cu) and five for Castle Sowerby (Cu).[2] Numbers fell rapidly as the process of enclosure became more formalised, more complex and more expensive. A memorandum to the Cartmel committee suggested that with more than three commissioners 'business seldom gets forward'.[3] While knowledge of local conditions was useful it could also be advantageous to have commissioners who, while skilled, were not acquainted with any of the landowners in a parish. This was the basis on which the Cartmel commissioners were chosen.[4] For many late eighteenth-century enclosures three commissioners were appointed, but instances of single commissioners are also known. From the first decade of the nineteenth century two commissioners became normal and after the General Enclosure Act of 1845 it was usual to have only one valuer. The men who were chosen as enclosure commissioners in north Lancashire and Westmorland were, as elsewhere, predominantly local, i.e. living within the same county. Commissioners could be drawn from further afield though while some Cumberland and Lancastrian commissioners are known to have worked in Yorkshire, including Thomas Wakefield of Yealand, one of the commissioners for the enclosure of Thornton in the West Riding (Table 4).[5] The qualities required in a commissioner were stated to be integrity, knowledge of the procedures involved, and sufficient fitness to cope with the rigours of the work.[6]

The occupation or social status of commissioners was generally recorded in the awards; over two-thirds of those for Westmorland and north Lancashire were styled 'gentleman' and a further 4.5 per cent 'esquire'. Others were estate stewards and land agents (a category which was dropped after 1801 because of potential partiality), land surveyors, clergymen and lawyers. Some men were of more modest station: Joseph Hodgson, commissioner for the enclosure of Stainton, Newbiggin and Blencow (Cu), was an ironmonger from Penrith.[7] Most of them were only involved in one or two awards, though some may, of course, have acted in other counties. Three Cumberland gentlemen are known to have undertaken a commission in the East Riding of Yorkshire.[8] Some of the commissioners who acted in Westmorland but came from Cumberland or Yorkshire may also have been active within their own counties. Most of them were only involved in one (65 per cent) or two (17 per cent)

Table 4. Geographical origins of north Lancashire and Westmorland enclosure commissioners.

	%
Westmorland	49
Cumberland	20
Yorkshire	11
Lancashire	17
Durham	1
Norfolk	1
London	1
Total	100

(Source: Enclosure awards)

Table 5. Social origins of Westmorland enclosure commissioners.

	%
Gentlemen	67
Esquire	4.5
Yeomen	3
Stewards & land agents	8
Land Surveyors	11
Clergymen	4.5
Lawyers	2
Total	100

(Source: Enclosure awards)

Table 6. Number of enclosure processes carried out by commissioners in north Lancashire and Westmorland.

No of Awards	%
1	65
2	17
3	4
4	3
5	3
6	2
7	3
8	0
9	2
25	1
Total	100

(Source: Enclosure awards)

awards, which might suggest a high level of inexperience among the commissioners, but 10 per cent dealt with between 5 and 10 awards and 1 per cent with 25. The most active were Thomas Heelis and Crayston Webster. Webster, as sole valuer for 25 enclosures made under the 1845 act, oversaw the re-shaping of some 17 per cent of the total area enclosed in Westmorland and 18 per cent in north Lancashire (Maps 7 & 8). This pattern is broadly similar to the work of commissioners in other areas. In the case of the East Riding, however, while 55 per cent only acted once there was a much larger group who had served on 30, 40 or even 50 enclosure commissions.[9]

Little information is available regarding the reasons behind the choice of particular men as commissioners. In 1801 the House of Commons Standing Orders stipulated that no one who was the land agent or estate steward of a proprietor who had an interest in a particular enclosure should be appointed as a commissioner,[10] something which effectively ended the enclosure career of men like Thomas Heelis, the Earl of Thanet's steward at Appleby Castle, whose only known work of this kind after 1801 was as overseer of the privately-arranged conversion of Dufton Fell into a stinted pasture. At Shap in 1805 new commissioners were chosen by a majority of the proprietors, by value of property, but at Bolton in 1803 the lord of the manor, Sir Frederick Vane, was recorded as having said that he expected to have the right to nominate one commissioner, as was then customary.[11] On the other hand, at Reagill in

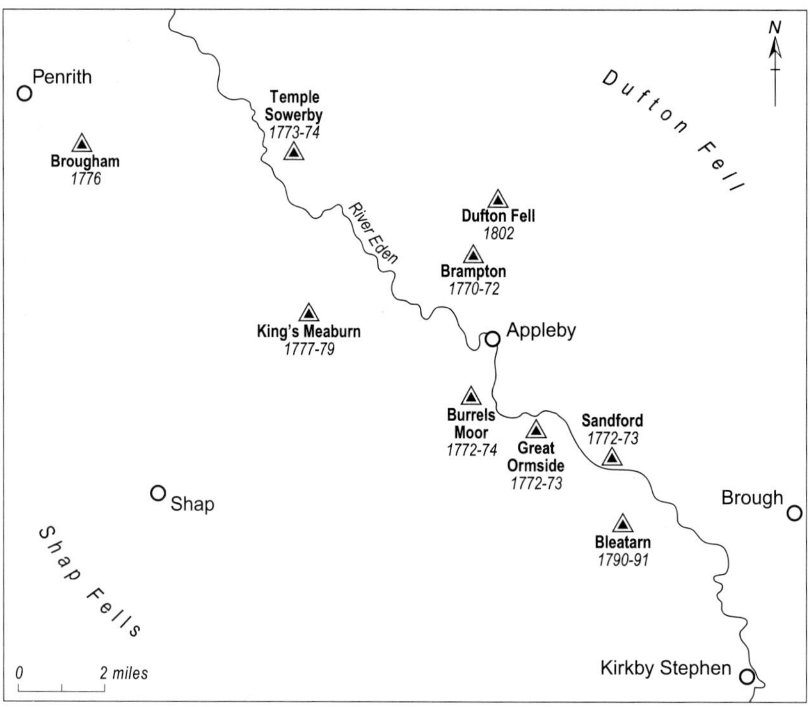

Map 7. The distribution of enclosures in which Thomas Heelis of Appleby Castle was a commissioner. Map drawn by Chris Beacock.

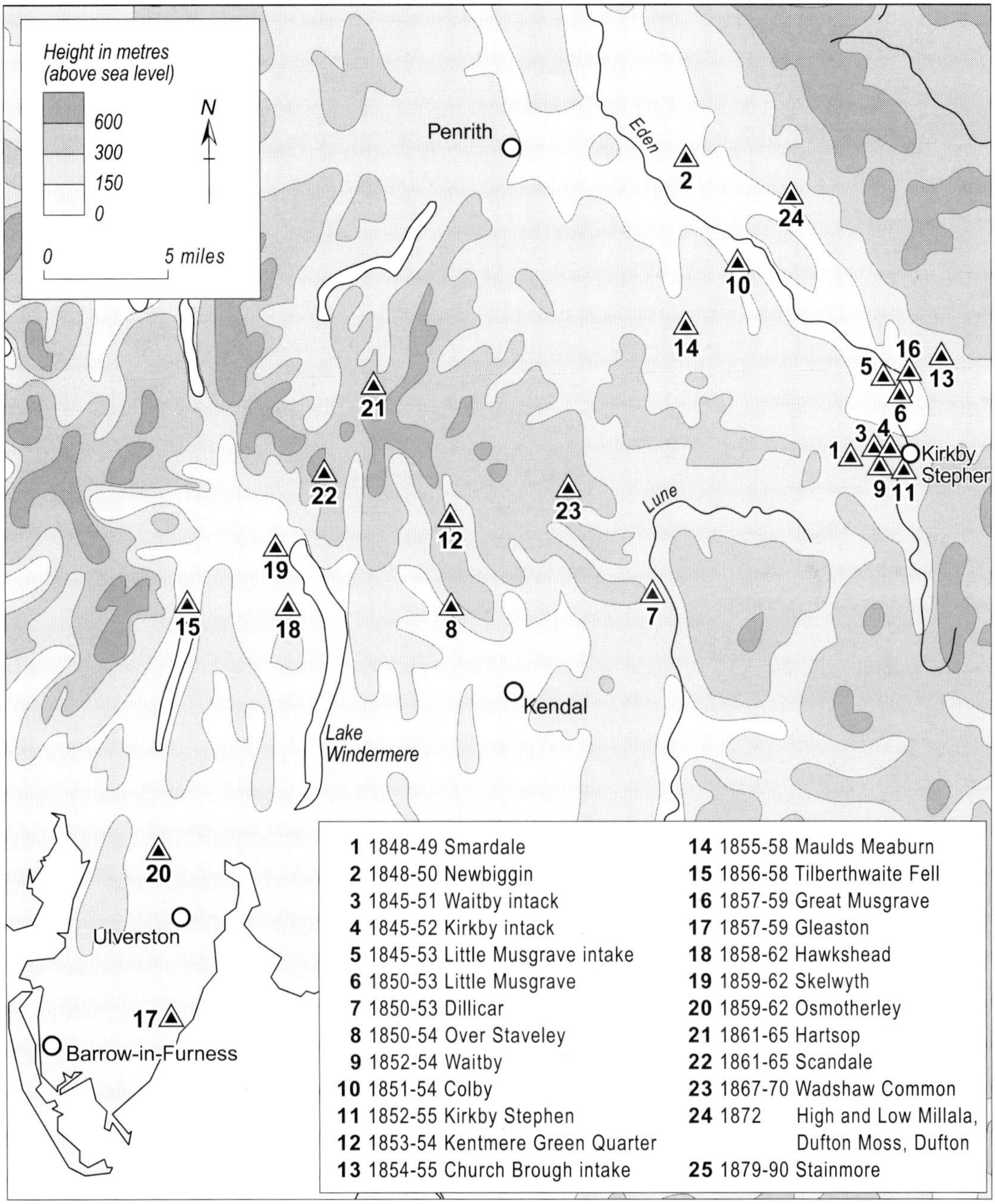

Map 8: Enclosures in which Crayston Webster, land surveyor of Kendal, was involved. Map drawn by Chris Beacock.

1802 Thomas Harrison was proposed as 'commissioner for the tenants'.[12] At Cartmel in 1795 one commissioner was nominated on behalf of the lord of the manor and the Bishop of Chester, while the remaining two were proposed by the landowners forming the committee who drew up the bill.[13] At Broughton in Furness (La) in 1839, when the original commissioner had died, a meeting was held at which two candidates were put forward to succeed him. John Slater received 33 votes from the proprietors who attended the meeting, his rival Martin Durham, a mere three votes. The process was, seemingly, a democratic one though it may be significant that Slater, who won so convincingly, was proposed by the lord of the manor.[14] At Hornby (La) it was stipulated that if a commissioner died, his successor was to be appointed by a majority of landowners of not less than two-thirds value of the land tax. Perhaps in part because of the problems caused with a few enclosures like Orton, a good deal of care was taken to ensure that the men chosen to act as commissioners had no direct, or even indirect, interest in the land being enclosed. John Beatham was dropped as a possible commissioner for Reagill as he had an interest in the adjoining townships of Sleagill and Newby, the boundaries of whose commons with Reagill were then in dispute.[15] The appointment of people without any interest in the land to be enclosed was taken seriously even at a lower level. At Dufton (We) one man was turned down for any work which involved estimating the quality of land because he had an interest in the common being enclosed. The commissioner decided that he could only be employed on work which involved surveying and staking out allotments.[16]

It is not clear how often efforts were made to try and influence commissioners' decisions. One case is described in a letter from Edward Jackson, commissioner for Dufton, who described how John Ellwood, one of those due to be allocated an allotment, came to see him to try and make some deal regarding the division of the common. Jackson stated that he was determined to stick to the letter of the law; 'it is impossible for me... to agree with any single individual. My agreement must be with the whole of the proprietors'.[17]

In return for their work, commissioners received a fixed fee per day; a guinea in the 1770s rising to two guineas by c.1800 and three in the early nineteenth century. Surveyors generally received a rate per acre: eight pence per acre at Helsington (We) in 1838 and a shilling per acre at Mansergh (We) in 1837.

Problems arose as to whether land which had been lost to a common in the past by piecemeal encroachment should be allowed to count in the award of an allotment. Encroachments that had been made within the previous 20 years were generally regarded as part of the common but in some cases, as at Ellel (La) in 1756 and Skelton (Cu) in 1769, those established as long ago as 40 years were not accepted as giving entitlement to an allotment.[18] In Cartmel, encroachments made over 20 years before, or those made within 20 years where a payment had been given to the parish sidesmen, were confirmed in possession but occupiers were not entitled to receive an allotment.[19] Where the allotments received were too small to be of much use there was often a provision that groups of smallholders could have their allotments amalgamated into one block in which they had proportional shares, as was done at Halton (La) in 1800 and Mungrisedale (Cu) in 1893 for five people whose allotments had ranged from just under half an acre (0.2ha) to a mere three perches.[20]

The timetable of events relating to any enclosure, though complex, was fairly standardised and was regulated by Parliament. Once the original discussions and negotiations regarding the desirability of enclosing an area of common had taken place and a decision had been made, from 1774 those involved had to place notices stating their intention of bringing a bill before Parliament on the doors of the local parish church or chapel and in local newspapers. A lot of work, only occasionally recorded, was put in at this stage by the proposed commissioners or, as at Cartmel, members of the enclosure committee, riding around the district, writing letters, or hanging around on market days trying to get as many proprietors as possible to agree to enclosure and to sign a petition in favour of it. There was also a lot of consultation between local solicitors and London legal experts. In the case of the bill from Cartmel the first printed version produced in London had clauses from the original draft omitted and new ones inserted so that the document was very different from the one to which the Cartmel landowners had originally agreed. The bill had to be withdrawn and it took two weeks to alter it so that it almost ran out of parliamentary time.[21] The petition was then submitted to Parliament asking leave to bring in a bill. The bill itself was usually presented to Parliament by a local MP. Petitions against it might also be made at this stage.

Once the act had been passed the commissioners could get to work in earnest. Their first and subsequent public meetings were advertised by notices fixed to the doors of local churches and chapels, as well as advertisements placed in newspapers. Meetings were almost invariably held in local inns within or close to the manor, parish or township concerned. This, as records of money spent on ale as part of the commissioners' expenses testify, suggests that the meetings may have been quite convivial but inns were important centres for meeting people and transacting business at this period. At the first meeting the commissioners took oaths to do their work honestly and impartially. Quakers merely made an affirmation. It was normal to appoint other officials, including the surveyor and a clerk to the commissioners, who was usually a local lawyer. Enclosure proceedings must have been a steady source of income to many country solicitors at this time. Sometimes an arbiter or umpire was also appointed, or elected by a majority of the commoners, to judge the claims to common rights and to settle any disagreements between the commissioners, also a banker to handle the money paid by the proprietors.

The first major piece of business for the commissioners was to make a boundary perambulation with local people to determine the precise limits of the common and establish if there were disagreements over them with neighbouring communities. Any disputes over the boundaries which the commissioners could not sort out might go to the local Quarter Sessions for resolution. At the second and third public meetings those who believed that they had rights to the use of a common were required to present written claims. Evaluating these claims, and any objections to them, might take a good deal of time but they had to be settled before work on allocating allotments could be started. This must have been one of the hardest task faced by commissioners. Unfortunately, details of those making claims and the basis on which they were accepted or rejected, rarely survive. In theory there was a greater chance of problems arising over claims where land was bring granted in lieu of common rights than with the enclosure of open arable fields where areas of land were simply being exchanged, because of the problem of clearly defining common rights. The complexity is illustrated by a list of claims to common rights drawn up for the Quernmore (La) enclosure. 119 claims were made of which 70 – over half – were rejected wholly or in part. One might have expected larger landowners and customary tenants to have found it easier to establish their claims, and that smallholders would have tended to lose out. The disallowed claims at Quernmore did include some substantial farmers as well as cottagers, but of the 47 claimants who had no land or under an acre, 43 had their claims turned down.[22] The thoroughness of the commissioners' work in this case is shown by the way in which some claims were allowed in part for some lands or property but were rejected for others.[23] The surveyor would then undertake a survey of the common, and a valuation of the old enclosures and other lands which formed the basis of claims to allotments. For very large areas more than one surveyor might be appointed. At Cartmel (La) four surveyors each had specified districts of the parish and their work was extended to include the planning of drainage schemes.[24] In some of the earlier enclosures, such as Orton, the quality of the maps produced by the surveyors was not particularly good but by the end of the eighteenth century the standards of detail and accuracy had improved, despite the fact that the rugged terrain involved in some cases cannot have made surveying easy.

Once the basic survey had been completed, the boundaries of the new allotments would be defined on the ground by lines of stakes, as would the courses of the new access roads, both public and private. Commissioners ensured, as far as possible, that the allotments they allocated were contiguous with existing holdings. To achieve this the largest allotments, generally those granted to the lord of the manor and tithe owner, were sometimes sited in relatively remote locations, as at Broughton in Furness (La) where the name 'Lord's High Allotment' is still marked on the 1:25,000 OS map. However, with the need to allocate land in terms of quality as well as quantity, and where the shape of a common was long and narrow, as at Knock (We), this was not always possible to achieve. It was not uncommon for landowners to receive their allotments in two or three separate blocks. Local people were given the opportunity to object if they did not like the alignment of any of the new enclosure roads. The sites for public quarries and watering places would also be identified. Contracts would be issued for making up the roads, and for ring-fencing the manorial and tithe allotments. Individual landowners could choose to undertake the fencing of their own allotments themselves or to pay local tradesmen to undertake the work. Allotment holders had to contribute to the cost of ring fencing the manorial and tithe allotments and were required to erect boundaries around their own allotments within a specified period.

Manorial lords did well out of enclosure; in return for relinquishing some of their traditional rights over the commons, which in practice may not have been worth very much, and for enfranchising their customary tenants by allowing them to become freeholders, they were granted allotments amounting in many cases to a sixteenth and sometimes a twelfth of the area. In the case of the Castle Sowerby (Cu) enclosure the lord of the manor received a full eighth of the land.[25] Despite this they usually retained the right to work minerals on other allotments provided that they paid suitable compensation for any inconvenience or damage caused. The church also did well in many cases, receiving a share often of an eighth or a twelfth in return for extinguishing the right to tithes from the enclosed land. As well as manorial and tithe allotments, small areas of land were also sometimes set aside for the use of various institutions; to the overseers of the poor, or the local grammar school. The 1845 General Enclosure Act, concerned about the loss of village greens as communal space, stipulated that land should be allocated in enclosures for recreation or village sports. Sometimes, as at New Hutton (We), the recreation allotment was well away from the village. In other cases it was combined with a gravel pit or quarry, as at Mansergh and Lupton (We).[26] At Lupton, the four-acre recreation allotment was known (tongue in cheek?) as the Pleasure Ground and annual village sports meetings were held there.[27]

On the Strickland Roger enclosure of 1853 the unfenced four-acre (1.6ha) recreation allotment is marked by four boundary stones at the corners, and a small plaque commemorating the granting of this plot of land to the community. Given that about half the allotment is marsh one wonders what kinds of recreation actually took place on this high-lying, remote area (Figure 10). Most charity allotments were small but at Culgaith (Cu) 100 acres (40.5ha) was granted to support the poor.[28]

The enclosure of the commons in one manor, parish or township could have unexpected effects on surrounding communities whose

Figure 10: The boundary stone marks a corner of the four-acre recreation allotment at Strickland Roger.

commons remained unenclosed. An account of Crosby Ravensworth parish, published in 1802, referred to the isolated thinly-inhabited township of Birkbeck Fells and how, following the recent enclosure of a nearby parish (surely Orton), their peat mosses had suffered severely from the depredations of those of their neighbours who no longer had rights to cut fuel.[29]

Not surprisingly, enclosure prompted a lot of property changes. People often sold their common rights in advance of enclosure, or disposed of their allotment once it had been staked out. Exchanges between allotment holders sometimes occurred while the sale of part of the enclosed land to cover costs offered another opportunity for existing landowners to expand their estates of people from outside the community to buy into it.

2. *The costs of enclosure*

The process of parliamentary enclosure was expensive, often more expensive than expected. There were even instances, such as Leck Fell (La), where the enclosure process cost more than the land was actually worth, and despite much of it being sold off additional funds had to be raised from reluctant proprietors to pay off the debt. A similar situation arose with Preston Patrick (We) where even 30 years after enclosure all the bills had not been paid off.[30]

The costs of enclosing former common pasture were probably greater than for open-field arable because of the additional expense of land improvement. On the other hand the increase in the rental value of the land was proportionally greater. Where land of reasonable quality was converted to arable the cost of enclosure could be paid off in two or three years.[31] The costs of enclosure included the initial expenses of drawing up the petition and the bill, getting them signed and then seeing the bill through Parliament, the fees paid to commissioners and other officers, the expenses involved in holding meetings to determine claims, undertaking the survey, staking out the allotments, making the new roads, ring fencing the manorial and tithe allotments, and finally drawing up the awards and making copies of it. On top of this were the individual costs of ring fencing each allotment, in some cases sub-dividing the allotments into smaller fields, improving the land and sometimes constructing new outbuildings or entire farmsteads on them.

In the earlier part of the period in particular many of the up-front costs of getting an enclosure bill and then an act through Parliament might be met by loans from major proprietors. At Cartmel £1,200 had to be raised to meet the costs of getting the bill through Parliament. Six landowners advanced £200 each, another £800 was added by James Stockdale and a further £1,352 10s. 0d. was raised to allow the commissioners to proceed with their work. The total public costs were nearly £17,000, a large sum in its day.[32] At Temple Sowerby (We) George Atkinson received an additional 15 acres of land in lieu of the money he had put up for defraying the cost of procuring the act. In the longer term, costs could be met by a proportional levy on all those receiving allotments. If costs exceeded the initial levy, a second one might be necessary, as at Dufton (We) in 1828, where the first rate of £712 9s. 0d. had to be supplemented by a larger one of £1,035 2s. 11d.[33] At Cliburn, a third levy had to be raised.[34] Alternatively, money could be raised by selling plots of former common land to the highest bidders. This was done in roughly half the awards in north west England.[35] The proportion of the land auctioned in this way was often around 10 per cent but ranged from as low as 4 per cent to over 50 per cent depending on the quality of the land involved.

Figures for the costs of enclosure are only available in a few cases. If it is assumed that the money raised from the sale of land was approximately equal to the total public costs of enclosure then this sum, which is available for more enclosure processes, can be used as a rough guide to costs. Income from sales of land in relation to the acreage enclosed could vary widely, even at the same period. There was no marked trend for public costs, measured in this way, to rise over time. Indeed, costs per acre tended to be higher during the Napoleonic Wars than in the mid-nineteenth century. This may be explained in part by the General Enclosure Acts of 1836 and 1845 streamlining the process and reducing costs per acre. Land enclosed in the mid or later nineteenth century, often of relatively poor quality, was often allotted in a few large blocks so that infrastructure costs were reduced. On the other hand there was a clear relationship between the cost of enclosure per acre and the number of years intervening between the dates of the act and award. As lengthy enclosure processes tended to be concentrated during the Napoleonic Wars, costs per acre then were often higher than later in the nineteenth century. Among the public costs some expenses, such as making the roads, were relatively easy to determine and could be forecast fairly accurately, but where an award dragged on other expenses such as legal fees and payments to commissioners might rise sharply. The amount of money raised from the sale of land sometimes proved insufficient to cover the final costs, necessitating an additional levy on those awarded allotments. Less commonly too much money was raised and repayments had to be made as at Egton with Newland (La) where the commissioners found that they had £2,066 left over when all the bills had been paid. They reimbursed this to the proprietors according to the sizes of their allotments, ranging from £152 2s. 1d. to the Duchess of Buccleuch to 4s. 1d. to Henry Shaw.[36] The sale of land was not always successful. At Dufton the majority of the ten plots offered for sale were not taken because they were located in part of the common which was the subject of a dispute over the right to cut turf as underlay for the thatch of houses in Dufton village.[37]

Information on the public costs of enclosure is available where commissioners accounts have survived. The Berrier (Cu) award of 1796 involved a total cost of £576 of which £160 went on obtaining the act, £200 on paying the commissioners' expenses, and £216 on the cost of the surveys and making the roads.[38] The additional costs of land improvement are also difficult to determine. Drystone walling cost around four shilling per rood of seven yards in the later eighteenth and early nineteenth centuries. By 1845 this had risen to eight shillings.[39] But this does not seem to have included the costs of quarrying or transporting the stones. At Arkholme in 1802 it cost the Trustees of Sedbergh School £60 15s. 0d. to fence their share of the boundary of a 21 acre (8.5ha) allotment, including the cost of carriage.[40] Hawthorn saplings for hedging cost around 15 shillings per 100 during the Napoleonic Wars[41] but the total cost of a hedge included ditching, and setting up protective post-and-rail fences to protect the young hedge plants from grazing animals. Overall there was probably not much difference in the total costs for hedging and walling the same length of boundary. Although some walling and hedging accounts survive it is probable that much of the work was done by family labour on the small farms which characterised so much of the area.

Once allotments had been fenced there was further expense. Liming the soil to reduce acidity might require 100–160 cartloads per acre at a shilling a load.[42] Paring off and burning the surface vegetation and turf, another form of improvement, could cost 12 to 16 shillings per acre.[43]

The expense of improving land from waste, including the removal of stones, liming and ploughing, was rarely less than £2 to £3 per acre and might well be £7 or more.[44] If a new steading was required then this might cost, in addition, several hundred pounds.[45] A number of enclosure awards contained the provision that those receiving allotments could opt to receive less land in return for having it ring-fenced at no cost to them.[46] Awards also indicted with great care which boundaries specific allotment holders were required to fence at their own cost – with luck it might only be about half of the perimeter of their new land.

Where money was raised by a levy on landowners in proportion to the amount of property they held, payments were sometimes slow to come in and it might take years for the commissioners to finally wind up their accounts. Although the enclosure of Preston Patrick (We) was probably completed around 1818 (there is no surviving award) the commissioners were still sending standard letters to landowners requesting payments in 1832.[47]

3. *Problems with enclosure*

A feature of parliamentary enclosure over England as a whole was that those processes carried out before the 1790s tended to take less time (one to three years between act and award) while later ones often took longer; five, six seven years or even more.[48] In part this may have been because the less contentious cases were tackled first while the more difficult ones were left until later. It has also been suggested that, during the Napoleonic Wars, commissioners may have deliberately dragged the enclosure process out in order to claim higher fees.[49] In general terms, however, a feature of parliamentary enclosure in the north west was the lengthy period often needed to complete enclosure processes compared with lowland England where relatively few enclosures took more than four or five years to accomplish. Chapman has suggested that in Wales, where parliamentary enclosure was also predominantly of upland waste, a much higher proportion of acts took a long time to complete compared with lowland England due to inexperience on the part of the commissioners.[50] In the north west as a whole 40 per cent of awards took more than five years to complete. In Westmorland 54 per cent of enclosures took five years or more to complete and 25 per cent ten years or more (Tables 7 & 8). Some of the delay may have been due to the large amount of land involved and the high numbers of claimants but the relationship between the time taken and the area enclosed, while positive, is not a strong one suggesting that other factors were involved.

Almost all late-eighteenth century enclosures were completed quickly. An exception was Orton (We) which took ten years due to problems in the way that the enclosure was handled. It may be that these late-

Table 7. Period of time between act and award in Cumbria and north Lancashire.

Period of time	Proportion of acts & awards	
	All enclosures %	Enclosures where land was sold %
Under 5 years	60	45
6–9	18	26
10–14	12	16
15–19	6	10
20+	4	3
Total	100%	100%

(Source: Enclosure awards)

Table 8. Average length of time taken between act and award per decade (years)

	Cumberland	Westmorland	N.Lancs	Total area
1750s			1.0	1.0
1760s	1.7	10.0		2.8
1770s	2.6	1.4	1.0	1.9
1780s	1.2			1.2
1790s	2.5	1.0	8.3	5.5
1800s	7.3	10.7	8.3	7.6
1810s	5.8	7.2	5.3	6.2
1820s	7.4	6.5	9.5	7.7
1830s	8.5	14.9		13.6
1840s	8.6	5.2		6.9
1850s	2.9	2.3	3.9	3.4
1860s	5.6	6.1		5.8
1870s	3.0	21.0		17.0
1880s	5.0			5.0
1890s	2.0			2.0

(Source: Enclosure awards)

eighteenth century cases were simply not contentious ones, especially as most of them involved relatively small areas – hundreds rather than thousands of acres – and limited numbers of people. Or it may be that procedures were less complex at this date and took less time to complete. During the war years and the 1820s 53 per cent of enclosures in the north west took over five years to finish. From the 1850s onwards the figure was much lower: (21 per cent). It is likely that the provisions of the 1845 General Enclosure Act allowed enclosure to proceed much faster and more smoothly in most cases while the high agricultural prices which prevailed during the war years of the early nineteenth century may have made enclosures at this time more contentious. It is also possible that the post-1815 slump in prices may have delayed some awards due to allotment holders having more difficulty in raising funds to meet the costs of enclosure. This is suggested by the fact that in Westmorland the average period from act to award for enclosures started and completed between 1800 and 1815 was 6.0 years but for those started before 1815 and completed after that date the figure was 9.9 years. However, over a broader time span, lack of capital does not seem to have been a major cause of delay; there was little difference between the length of time taken for all enclosures and for those where land was sold to cover costs (Table 7).

On the other hand much of the enclosure activity in Westmorland and Lancashire north of the sands during the 1770s and after 1845 was dominated by a small number of highly professional commissioners. The two most notable, as we have seen, were Thomas Heelis and Crayston Webster. None of Heelis' nine awards and only three out of Webster's 25 took more than five years to complete. This may indeed imply that a lack of experience by other commissioners slowed down progress. The causes of such delays are not always possible to identify where only the award has survived or even where supplementary documentation, including minute books, accounts and correspondence, exists.

One factor which could delay an enclosure was the death of one or more of the commissioners. Given the need to used experienced, mature men and the fact that completing an award often took several years, it was not uncommon for a commissioner to die in office. Where an active commissioner was working on a number of awards simultaneously, this could cause widespread problems. The cases of Reagill and Shap (We), where all the commissioners died without appointing successors and new acts had to be secured, have already been mentioned. Cases of commissioners resigning and being replaced also occur such as Robert Lumb of Lowther who resigned from two sets of enclosure proceedings, Casterton and Scalthwaiterigg (We), in 1812 and Bryan Gray who resigned from the Over Kellet (La) enclosure in 1797 'through indisposition'. More exotically, enclosure of the common of Warcop (We) was held up because the commissioner had gone off to Potosi in South America, famous for its silver mines!

Lack of experience on the part of commissioners is difficult to identify. The Rev. Edward Jackson, vicar of Bolton (We), who was commissioner for the enclosure of Dufton (We) from 1827, confessed himself to be diffident and unsure of his abilities[51] but cases of incompetence are hard to spot. A study of the parliamentary enclosure of Saddleworth in the Pennines, where the act was passed in 1810 but the award was only made in 1834, indicated that delays were due to a variety of factors including the complex nature of the claims to rights on the common due to the earlier history of enclosure in this area, the time taken to deal with the many encroachments which had been made on the moor, delays due to problems in defining the boundary of the common, the slowness of the surveyors, commitments elsewhere which resulted in the commissioner rarely being in attendance at certain periods and finally the death of the original commissioner.[52] The surviving documentation for this enclosure is more detailed than for any of the parliamentary enclosure processes in Westmorland or north Lancashire. As a result it provides insights into the kinds of difficulties which may have arisen further north. However, there is much less evidence in the north west of commissioners being involved in large numbers of awards simultaneously, as was the case in the East Riding of Yorkshire.[53]

A common problem was boundary disputes. Disagreements over the boundaries of townships and manors in north west England continued, in some cases, to the end of the nineteenth century.[54] The fact that intercommoning between manors or townships, with complex sets of customary rights, continued so late helps to account for this. In the huge parish of Cartmel (La), prior to the enclosure act of 1796, there was no definition, indeed no clear knowledge, of the boundaries of the various townships within the parish where they crossed common land.[55] The boundaries of commons (usually also the manorial boundaries) were sometimes defined by streams (fairly clear unless their courses shifted), watersheds (sometimes less distinct), stone cairns, or currocks and less frequently by man-made boundaries like ditches and banks.[56] Sometimes the inhabitants of one community might use the commons of another in return for a small payment, thus establishing rights which might have to be seriously considered at enclosure. In this way the people of Great and Little Asby (We) acquired a share of turbary rights on Orton common amounting to 269 and 168 acres (109 & 70ha) respectively.

From 1801 enclosure commissioners had the power, where the boundaries of a common were uncertain, to examine witnesses, weigh up the evidence and make a ruling regarding the course of the boundary. In the event of this being disputed, cases could be referred to the local Quarter Sessions. Where the boundary between two commons was irregular commissioners also had the power to straighten it by agreement with the other community to reduce the cost of fencing. They might even get the other community to pay for part of the cost. In the case of a disputed boundary between the commons of Reagill and Sleagill (We) in 1803, eyewitness evidence given to the commissioners extended back to the 1730s while documentary evidence from the seventeenth century was also cited.[57] This was all to no avail for agreement could not be reached and the case went to the Quarter Sessions at Appleby. There do not seem to have been any major boundary disputes associated with the late eighteenth century enclosures. One associated with the Brampton (We) enclosure of 1772 between landowners in the township and the borough of Appleby seems to have been quickly resolved. The fact that most of the commons were relatively small and probably intensively-used areas of lowland pasture, whose boundaries ought to have been well known, may help to account for this. From 1801 until 1806, which is as far as the Westmorland Quarter Sessions rolls have been indexed, a number of cases of boundary disputes prompted by enclosure arose. Such disputes are not necessarily evident from the wording of the enclosure awards and are more likely to emerge where other supplementary papers have survived. In other cases the existence of ruler-straight boundaries dividing the commons of adjoining townships suggests late readjustment by enclosure commissioners.

A well-recorded boundary dispute arose in 1814 concerning the townships of Preston Patrick and Lupton (We) east of Kendal.[58] Evidently it was the perambulation of the boundary by the commissioners that set off the dispute though the depositions of witnesses suggest that there had been friction in the past over who had rights to grazing and cutting turves in specific areas. The accounts record payments for writing summonses for witnesses to give evidence to the commissioners and expenses of five shillings per day for those who attended. Four days were taken up by this in August and September 1814.[59] The issue was not a straightforward one because witnesses revealed cases where farmers with holdings in Preston Patrick had, at various times, owned or leased land in Lupton, giving them rights to the use of both commons. A surviving sketch survey shows that the boundary was disputed over a considerable length but not a great width. The topography of the area encouraged confusion; the irregular line of the watershed was far from clear among several low hills and marshy saddles (Figure 11). The case went to the Quarter Sessions in Appleby and seems to have been resolved by 1818.

In the case of Preston Patrick enclosure precipitated a boundary dispute. In other instances, however, disagreements over boundaries could delay enclosure. This is demonstrated by the example of the commons of Smardale, Waitby and Kirkby Stephen (We), running back in long narrow strips with Kirkby Stephen common extending far up the slope of Wild Boar Fell. Because of the shapes of the commons, the areas in dispute accounted for a substantial proportion of their total extent. It was only after an agreed boundary award had been made by the tithe commissioners in the mid-1840s that enclosure became feasible, with awards being made between 1849 and 1855.[60] The enclosure of the commons of Dent and Garsdale (Yo) likewise seem to have been delayed until a dispute over mutual boundaries, as well as ones with Barbon and Middleton (We), had been sorted out by the tithe commissioners.[61] In some areas the complexity of boundary claims was considerable. In the

Figure 11: The course of the boundary between Preston Patrick and Lupton which was eventually agreed between the commissioners and the landowners: there is a small quarry for walling stone in the foreground.

featureless moorlands which lie south of Stainmore, between Nine Standards Rig and Tan Hill, the boundaries of the townships of Kaber, Winton and Hartley in Westmorland and Birkdale, Ravenseat and Stonesdale in Yorkshire were contested over a large area.[62] In some cases the settling of boundary disputes by the Tithe Commissioners in the 1840s may have had as significant effect as the General Enclosure Act of 1845 in reducing the costs of enclosure.

4. *The enclosure of Orton*

A complicated dispute arose in connection with the enclosure of Orton (We). The circumstances were unique and it is hard to judge to what extent inexperience, cupidity or a combination of the two were to blame. Orton and Raisbeck were separate manors within the parish of Orton. The customary tenants of each manor had bought the manorial rights in the early seventeenth century. Following this separate manorial courts continued to be held to prevent encroachments and to regulate the commons. At some time in the early eighteenth century the two courts were amalgamated in order to save money and were held jointly at Orton. In the mid-late eighteenth century the inhabitants of Orton allowed the encroachment of a number of cottages on parts of their common adjoining Raisbeck and a considerable amount of peat cutting also reduced the value of the Orton commons. The Raisbeck commons, twice the size of the ones in Orton and of comparable quality, were also starting to come under pressure (Figure 12).

When support for an enclosure bill was being canvassed most of the inhabitants of Orton were in favour and most in Raisbeck against. Of the three commissioners appointed in 1769 to undertake the Orton enclosure one already held land in Orton and another bought land there after the act was passed. Two of the three commissioners thus had a direct interest in the proceedings, an unusual and undesirable situation. The 1769 act made no mention of the manor of Raisbeck but in 1773, when the commissioners started work in earnest, it was soon realised that they were setting out allotments on Raisbeck, as well as Orton, commons. The inhabitants of Raisbeck protested to the commissioners and took legal advice. As a result of the upset this caused, the commissioners seem to have done little for five years. In 1779 an award was made which included allotments on Raisbeck common. The advice of legal counsel was that Raisgill did not have a case because, first, they had allowed joint meetings of their manor court with Orton over a long period of time and earlier records of a separate court at Raisbeck had not survived. Second, the inhabitants of Raisbeck had acquiesced in this and, crucially, no protest had been made by any of the Raisbeck landowners when the commissioners had made the initial perambulation of the boundaries of the area to be enclosed, including their common, although public warning of the date of the meeting had been given. The inhabitants of Raisbeck were nevertheless still resisting the process of enclosure in 1782, three years after the award had been made. They were convinced that the commissioners were biased and that the whole affair was a ploy by the people of Orton to get a share of the Raisbeck commons; they may well have been right.[63]

Figure 12: Part of the former Raisbeck commons which the commissioners for the Orton enclosure were so keen to incorporate into their enclosure plan.

Relations between Orton and Raisbeck were further complicated by a dispute over the boundary between the two commons. The problems are detailed in a document which is undated but which, judging by the people mentioned, was written at around the time of the enclosure proceedings. As well as a disagreement over the line of the boundary there were differences of opinion over who had a right to graze livestock, cut turf and pull heather on Raisbeck common. Some inhabitants of Orton seem to have acquired small amounts of land in Raisbeck manor as a way of trying to gain access to the larger Raisbeck commons. Not surprisingly, the people of Raisbeck objected.[64]

It took some time for the new allotments to be completely assimilated with the older improved lands. At Arkholme (La), the farm of Deepmire was still being advertised as 54 acres (22ha) of ancient enclosed land and a 21 acre (8.5ha) allotment of common in 1832, nearly 30 years after the enclosure award.[65] The distinctiveness of the allotments was due in large measure to the character of the new enclosure landscapes and it is to this topic that we now turn.

Notes

1. LRO DDCa 27/14/24.
2. CRO (Barrow) BDX 278/3 & 4.
3. LRO DDCa 22/14/14.
4. LRO DDCa 22/14/26.
5. S. Hollowell, *Enclosure Records for Historians* (Phillimore, 2000), p.8.
6. LRO DDCa 22/14/1.
7. R.S. Dilley, 'The case of the Stainton, Newbiggin and Blencow enclosure award'. *TCWAAS* Series 2 95 (1995), pp.187–98.
8. J. Crowther, *Enclosure Commissioners and Surveyors of the East Riding* (East Yorkshire Local History Society, 1986).
9. *Ibid.*
10. P. Higson, 'Landlord control and motivation in the parliamentary enclosure of St. Mary's on-the-Hill parish, Chester', *Transactions of the Historic Society of Lancashire and Cheshire* 137 (1987), pp.93–116.
11. CRO (Kendal) WQ/R/I Bolton misc. enclosure papers.
12. CRO (Kendal) WQ/E/I Reagill misc. enclosure papers.
13. LRO DDCa 22/14/26.
14. CRO (Barrow) BCP/1.
15. *Ibid.*
16. CRO (Kendal) WD/HH/53 Dufton misc. enclosure papers.
17. *Ibid.*
18. A.B. Humphries, 'Agrarian Change in East Cumberland, 1750–1900', Unpublished M.Phil.Thesis, University of Lancaster, 1993, p.163.
19. Stockdale, *Annals of Cartmel*, p.327.
20. Humphries, Agrarian Change, p.216.

21. LRO DDCa 27/14/26.
22. LRO DDX 70/29.
23. *Ibid.*
24. Stockdale, *Annals of Cartmel*, p.330.
25. CRO (Barrow) BDX 278/3.
26. A. Hall, 'The Role of Village Greens in Westmorland', Unpublished MA Dissertation, University of Lancaster, 2001, p.46; B.L. Thompson, *Some Westmorland Villages* (Westmorland Federation of Women's Institutes, 1957), p.102; R.S. Dilley, 'The enclosure awards of Cumberland: a statistical list', *TCWAAS* Series 2 100 (2000), p.275.
27. Thompson, *Westmorland Villages*, p.102.
28. Dilley, Cumberland Awards, p.225.
29. J.T. Relph, *Chronicles of Crosby Ravensworth* (1992).
30. Select Committee on Commons Inclosure 1844 (Command paper 583) vol 5, p.133.
31. F.W. Garnett, *Westmorland Agriculture 1800–1900* (Titus Wilson, 1912), p.54; Select Committee on Inclosure, vol 5
32. Stockdale, *Annals of Cartmel*, p.329.
33. CRO Kendal WD/HH/53.
34. CRO (Kendal) WQR/I.
35. Dilley, Cumberland Awards, p.225.
36. LRO DDX 116/81.
37. CRO (Kendal) WD HH/53 Dufton misc. enclosure papers.
38. Humphries, Agrarian Change, p.183.
39. CRO (Kendal) WDX/1008; Garnett, *Westmorland Agriculture*, p55.
40. LRO DDX/3/12.
41. R.W. Dickson, *General View of the Agriculture of Lancashire* (1815), p.216.
42. *Ibid.*, p.452.
43. Garnett, *Westmorland Agriculture*, pp.55–57.
44. Dickson, *Agriculture of Lancashire*, p.198.
45. G.E. Mingay, *Parliamentary Enclosure in England: an introduction to its causes, incidence, and impact, 1750–1850* (Longman, 1998), p.111.
46. CRO (Kendal) WPR/47 Preston Patrick.
47. LRO WDX 247.
48. Mingay, *Parliamentary Enclosure*, p.21.
49. M. Turner, 'Enclosure commissioners and Buckinghamshire Parliamentary Enclosure', *Agricultural History Review* 25 (1977), pp.120–9.
50. J. Chapman, *A Guide to Parliamentary Enclosures in Wales* (University of Wales, 1992), pp.8–9.
51. CRO (Kendal) WQ/R/I Bolton misc. enclosure papers.
52. A.J. Petford, 'The process of enclosure in Saddleworth 1625–1834', *Transactions of the Antiquarian Society of Lancashire and Cheshire* 84 (1987), pp.78–117.
53. Crowther, *Enclosure Commissioners*.
54. A.J.L. Winchester, 'Dividing lines in a moorland landscape: territorial boundaries in upland England', *Landscapes* 1 (2) (2000), pp.23–24.
55. LRO DDCa 22/14/2.

56. A.J.L. Winchester, *The Harvest of the Hills* (Edinburgh University Press, 2000), p.29.
57. CRO (Kendal) WQ/R/I Reagill and Sleagill misc. enclosure papers.
58. CRO (Kendal) WDX/83/1–9.
59. CRO (Kendal) WDX/83/1–9.
60. CRO (Kendal) WD/HAL, 14a, 14b 16, 17.
61. CRO (Kendal) WPR/40.
62. CRO (Kendal) WD/HAL, 23, 27.
63. CRO (Kendal) WDX/194/1.
64. CRO (Kendal) WPR 9/Z 1–9, 13, 16–20.
65. CRO (Kendal) WDB 35.

CHAPTER SIX

Enclosure landscapes

In the last chapter we saw how enclosure commissioners operated at a local level to transform the landscape. In this chapter we look at the impact of this activity in changing the face of the countryside. We have already seen the amount of land involved for each county. Some individual enclosures covered huge areas. Inglewood Forest (Cu), between Carlisle and Penrith, was enclosed as a block of 28,000 acres (11,331ha) from 1819. Cartmel (La), the award for which was made in 1806, involved 12,760 acres (5,164ha). In such instances a single enclosure award could transform extensive areas of countryside. In other cases the amount of land involved was much more modest, and the landscape impact correspondingly small, such as the 89 acres (36ha) enclosed at Urswick (La) and the 49 acres (20ha) at Borwick (La), so that one is curious as to why the proprietors went to the expense of obtaining acts for such tiny areas and why they could not agree to private divisions.

The basic characteristic of a lowland parliamentary enclosure landscape, when seen from a prominent viewpoints such as Hartside Height, is that the countryside is more open without the density of hedgerows and trees often found among areas of older, smaller enclosures. Often there is a contrast between hedges bounding the old enclosures and stone walls on parliamentary-enclosed land. Areas of parliamentary enclosure are characterised by straight field boundaries, wide, straight roads and large fields, often square or rectangular. It is important to note, however, that similar landscapes could be created on land subject to privately-agreed enclosure or by the enclosure of demesne land under the direct management of a landowner, like the former deer park on Whinfell (Cu), near Penrith, which was enclosed into farms in 1767.[1]

Despite being laid out so meticulously by a surveyor's chain the character of the parliamentary-enclosure landscapes was strongly influenced by pre-existing features. The areas enclosed were defined by the irregular boundaries of the earlier commons, between the uphill limits of the old enclosures and the manorial, parish or township boundaries which, often following topographic features such as streams and watersheds, were also often winding and irregular. As we have seen, however, commissioners sometimes straightened out such boundaries. In upland areas especially, varied topography often made the adoption of a regular grid plan for allotments and access roads impossible. Layouts were most regular on land reclaimed from coastal salt marsh and peat moss, as in the Lyth valley (We), or where topography was fairly uniform, as in Inglewood Forest (Cu).

In lowland areas like the Eden valley, where much of the best land had already been taken into cultivation by the end of the eighteenth century, areas of surviving common sometimes only formed narrow strips on the fringes of townships such as King's Meaburn (We) (Figure 13). In upland manors, with more extensive areas of improvable waste, it was easier to set out allotments in large regular blocks. The easiest approach, where conditions were favourable, was to lay out a single straight access road with allotments running off on either side in square or rectangular blocks. However, the nature of the topography, the irregular shape of the area to be enclosed and the desire of landowners to have the new allotments, as far as possible, contiguous with their original holdings did not always permit this.

The manorial allotment, frequently the largest single block of land allocated by the commissioners, was often relatively remotely sited in order to give smaller allotment holders a better chance of having their new allotments contiguous, or at least fairly close, to their existing land, something which the commissioners took a good deal of trouble to arrrange as far as possible. The logic was that the manorial allotment was often large enough to support a totally new farm while this was much less likely to be the case with the smaller allotments of minor landowners and customary tenants

Awards sometimes contained detailed provisions regarding the precise location of walls and fences in relation to the boundaries staked on the ground.[2]

Figure 13: The narrow strip of common on the fringe of King's Meaburn township was only a single field wide when enclosed; it is still under cultivation today.

1. *Allotments and field boundaries*

Both hedges and stone walls were used in fencing allotments and their internal boundaries. On much of the low ground enclosed in the late eighteenth and early nineteenth century hawthorn hedges were used, as they were the quickest-growing shrub. This accounts for one version of their alternative name of 'quickthorn' though, according to the Oxford English Dictionary the word derives from 'quick' in the sense of 'living' – as opposed to the dry brushwood hedges which were common in medieval times.[3] Also, being so prickly, they formed a particularly effective barrier, but holly, hazel, elder, alder and willow were also planted. Hawthorns were sometimes raised locally but orders were often taken by travelling salesmen from Scottish nurseries. At Hoff and Drybeck (We) hedges were required to have 50 hawthorn plants per rood of seven yards.[4] It was normal to require sheep and goats to be kept out of new fields for seven or even ten years where hedges were used in order to prevent them from damaging the young hedge plants unless secure protective post and rail fences were erected on either side. Hedges often had trees planted in them at regular intervals – at Skelton (Cu) these were mainly oak and ash.[5] In the Eden valley there was a tradition of planting fruit trees – apple but also pear – at regular intervals in the hedges as well. The hedging accounts for the land allotted to New Hall Farm on the Sandford (We) award of 1773 include payment for crab apple as well as hawthorn saplings.[6] Hedges were not always planted carefully enough though; sometimes they were set on banks that were too high causing them to be too exposed and to suffer from drought.[7]

Stone walls were normally used on higher ground where hedges would not thrive and also on lower ground for most of the mid-nineteenth century awards. They were of fairly standard construction, differing from older walls in their use of less massive foundation stones, their frequent use of more angular quarried stone, and their construction with two outer faces, bonded together across a core of rubble by protruding courses of throughstones, with a line of capstones to shed water and protect the core from dampness (Figure 14). Earlier walls used throughstones but they did not stick out from the face of the wall, as did those in walls constructed from the middle of the eighteenth century.[8] Differences in the appearance of walls often relate as much to local geology as to variations in construction techniques. On the limestone moors around Shap (We), where large glacial erratics of Shap granite are widely scattered on the land surface, these have often been incorporated into the foundations of parliamentary enclosure walls. Many awards did not contain detailed stipulations relating to the construction of allotment walls but in some cases the height and width were specified as well as the number of courses of throughstones and the number of throughstones per rood of wall,

Figure 14: A parliamentary enclosure period drystone wall, Kirkby Stephen common: two courses of throughstones was more common than one, as shown here.

together with the minimum thickness of the wall at the base and the top. A height of six feet was a common stipulation. Details of the construction of the boundaries do not often survive but for Kirkby Stephen (We) a contract between a landowner and a waller exists which specifies that the ground forming the foundations for the wall was to be levelled, where necessary by cutting the turf away to a depth of six inches. The wall was to be six feet high, three-and-a-half feet wide at the base, 16 inches wide at the top, with a line of capstones set on edge and three courses of throughstones with not less than nine throughstones in each layer for each rood of wall.[9] At Arkholme (La), the trustees of Sedbergh School negotiated a contract with William Thompson of Halton to build 90 roods of wall to fence the boundary of their allotment. The wall was to be five feet high with at least another eight inches of coping stones. Two courses of throughstones with at least eight in each course for each rood of walling were also specified. The contract was agreed on 20 May 1802 and the wall was to be finished by 30 September. However, Thompson had still not completed 20 roods of the wall by the following February and the Trustees realised that this would probably not be completed until April 1803 as it would hardly be practicable to cart stones to the site before the end of March, presumably because the ground was too wet.[10]

Many enclosure walls are clearly lower than the stipulated height; often closer to four feet than six, either because of subsidence in soft ground or in an attempt to reduce construction costs and time. In such cases it has often been necessarily at a later time to increase the height of the barrier as a deterrent to sheep trying to climb over. Most commonly this has been done by driving in beside the wall a line of wooden posts with one or two strands of barbed wire above the level of the stonework

(Figure 15). On the enclosures around Dent (Yo) the wall has been heightened by the expedient of supporting a single strand of barbed wire on upright stones, sometimes notched for holding the wire, built up above the capstones, both stone and wire being attached to the wall by vertical wires which are anchored to the wall by running them through gaps in the stonework (Figure 16). Although the stone used for walling was mostly obtained from as close to the site as possible, stone gateposts were often made from easily-worked sandstone and might be brought in from some distance away.

Figure 15: An enclosure wall on the slopes of Wild Boar Fell with post and barbed wire added.

Figure 16: A more unusual way of raising the height of a wall in Dentdale.

There were two main sources of stone for walls; 'field' stones from the glacial drift, picked out of the allotments, and quarried stone. The former can be recognised in walls by having less angular, more rounded corners. They bonded less well than quarried stone but, where available, may often have involved less work to gather. Although landowners were allowed to take stone from the public quarries for constructing walls these were often some distance away. It was common for stone to be extracted from outcrops adjoining the wall, where the geology was suitable, or from specially-dug small quarry pits only a few yards away. These are often grassed over but still clearly visible.

Hedges had the advantage of costing less than stone walls initially[11] but it took a number of years for them to grow up into a stockproof barrier, during which period they had to be protected from damage by grazing animals. Stone walls might be more expensive to build but once finished were fully effective immediately, though maintenance costs increased over time. It was particularly important to ensure that allotment boundaries along the major roads were properly fenced and provisions in the awards sometimes specified this. The Quernmore, and Nether Kellet (La) awards stipulated that such boundaries had to be stone walls while other allotment boundaries could be walls or hedges. On some of the late nineteenth-century commons – like Mungrisedale (Cu) and Asby Scar (We) post and wire fencing was used (Figure 17). At

Figure 17: An original post and wire enclosure fence on the former Mungrisedale Common.

Mungrisedale some of the drilled slate pillars have the date of enclosure carved on them. At Asby iron posts are set into the bare limestone surface.

Internal boundaries were usually similar in character to the ring fences of the allotments and in most cases are likely to date from soon after the award. In some cases low banks of tumbled stones show where either an internal enclosure boundary has become redundant and has been deliberately demolished, or where stone has been gathered with the intention of constructing a boundary which was never in fact finished. The first edition of the OS 6-inch map from the late 1840s in Lancashire and the early 1860s in Cumberland and Westmorland may help to distinguish between the two types of case. If a wall is marked on the map at this time but is ruined today then it has probably been demolished subsequently but where no wall, or merely a dotted line is shown on the map then it is likely that the landowner ran out of enthusiasm, money, or both, particularly in the period following 1815 when agricultural prices slumped and much arable land reverted to pasture. An example can be seen on land enclosed under the Preston Patrick and Lupton awards (We). At Grid Reference SD559829 the boundaries of a shelter belt seem to have originally been planned to continue right up to the boundary between the two townships and then along it, but the work seems never to have been completed (Figure 18).

Figure 18: An unfinished shelter belt on the Preston Patrick enclosure: stones were collected but the protective wall was never completed.

Stone walls tended to be used at higher altitude and in more exposed situations where hedges would not thrive. However, there was a good deal of local variation. On the Great Ormside (We) enclosure of 1772, looking at the low ridge called Heights from the farm of Helm, one might at first think that the owners of the new later eighteenth-century allotments had planned their fencing logically with hedges on the low ground and walls higher up. However, as you walk through the area and examine the boundaries in detail you can find stray sections of walling among the hedges and vice versa. Continuing south over the crest of the hill you then find that the low ground on the other side is divided up by walls, not hedges. The decision

Figure 19: On the Great Ormside enclosure fences are a mixture of hedges and stone walls without any clear pattern.

making was clearly complex and not readily understandable today (Figure 19).

While the basic character of parliamentary enclosure walls is well known, detailed observation of the materials used, techniques of construction and relationships to earlier walls can provide further insights into enclosure history. This can be seen in the example of Nateby Cow Close (We), lying below Tailbridge Hill, south west of Kirkby Stephen. Nateby Cow Close was divided and enclosed in 1857 by private agreement, not parliamentary act.[12] However, it had originally been a stinted cow pasture, enclosed from the common before 1590.[13] An examination of its perimeter wall, dating from its creation as a stinted pasture, shows it to be relatively massive in structure with irregular foundations, made largely of field stones lifted from the glacial drift. The internal division walls, dating from the enclosure of 1857 are of classic parliamentary enclosure period construction with capstones, and throughstones, using quarried stone, not field stones (Figures 20 & 21).

Figures 20 & 21: Nateby Cow Close: the older outer wall, relatively crudely constructed from rounded field stones, contrasts with the neater wall of angular quarried stone dating from the nineteenth-century division.

Figure 22: Wall end at junction between townships of Weddicar (on left, enclosed 1809) and Whillimoor (on right, enclosed 1823) west Cumberland. Reproduced by kind permission of A.J.L. Winchester.

The junctions of walls, showing which one is the older, is a feature of some enclosures such as Weddicar and Whillimoor in west Cumberland (Figure 22).

2. *Quarries, roads and turbaries*

Virtually all awards set aside space for public quarries, including separate ones for limestone and freestone (sandstone) where the geology permitted, and sometimes pits for the extraction of sand and gravel. Commons had, of course, been a source of stone for centuries and some enclosure award maps mark existing quarries, as at Broughton in Furness High Moor. Enclosure acts and awards often specified the maximum area for all quarry plots: four acres (1.6ha) was common. Small areas of enclosure had only one quarry but for larger ones there were often several. The quarries were designed to provide material for making walls on the allotment boundaries and for the access roads which led to them. Allotment holders could also use the stone for other purposes such as making internal boundaries, outbuildings or even farmsteads, as long as it was for their own use. Gravel, sand and clay pits were also marked out by the commissioners in some cases. Awards sometimes required that the quarries should be worked in a regular way with waste being removed so that it did not obstruct the quarry face. On the Bleatarn (We) enclosure of 1791 little attention seems to have been paid to such stipulations. The entrance into the area set out by the commissioners for extracting stone is still clearly marked on the ground but the quarry itself is merely an area of irregular humps and bumps with no sign of a proper rock face at all (Figure 23). Many parliamentary enclosure quarries were small and seem to have been used for only a short period of time, although they are mostly still marked on modern maps. Others seem to have been in use over a longer period and are larger though very few are still being worked. Allotment owners could open their own quarries on their allotments. They often did this when the underlying rock as limestone, with adjacent kilns for burning lime for agricultural use. On the Casterton (We) enclosure they were specifically allowed to do this and in areas like Orton (We) virtually every farm had its own lime kiln on or adjoining the new allotment (Figure 24). Places for watering livestock, in streams, tarns and pools, were also provided by the commissioners, sometimes with facilities for washing sheep.

Figure 23: The allotment holders at Bleatarn seem to have paid little attention to the stipulations in the enclosure award that they should work their quarry neatly and carefully.

Figure 24: Field limekiln among the Orton enclosures.

One of the achievements of parliamentary enclosure was to improve farmers' access to local market centres by laying out networks of improved public and private roads between the allotments.[14] Enclosure roads were as important in this respect at a local scale as the turnpikes were at a regional level. Access roads could take up a significant proportion of the area of the former common. At Halton (La) where the area enclosed was 954 acres (386ha), nearly 21 acres (8.5ha) were accounted for by the new roads. At Scotforth (La) roads took up 37 of the 1,332 acres (15 of 590ha) dealt with by the commissioners. The quality of such roads was ensured by Parliament's requirement that they should be inspected and approved by a local Justice of the Peace.[15]

As was general elsewhere in England the main public roads laid out in the later eighteenth century were very wide – at least 60 feet – creating in limestone country some impressive flower-rich verges (Figure 25). At Brampton (We) the main road was 27 yards wide. From the 1790s, however, roads became narrower with 40 feet and later 30 feet as the normal maximum width (Figure 26).[16] The reasons for the great width of the earlier roads were more likely to relate to the provision of enough space for traffic to avoid wet or churned-up patches, and to ensure the easy movement of livestock, rather than creating a grazing reserve for

Figure 25: This 60-foot wide late eighteenth-century enclosure road at Skelton looks like an avenue leading to a country house.

Figure 26: A narrower 30-foot wide mid-nineteenth century enclosure road, Kirkby Stephen.

cottagers deprived of their common rights. At Orton the manorial court expressly forbade the grazing of livestock on the verges of its wide public roads. In 1861 the court decided that these were a waste of space and permitted landowners to encroach on them, leaving a minimum width, on payment of 50 shillings per acre.[17] Better road surfacing and more effective drainage with culverts seems to have been the principal factors allowing widths to be reduced. By the early nineteenth century the surveyors of highways appointed by the enclosure commissioners were using Macadam's technique of pounding small stones together until they interlocked to form an all-weather surface. At Cartmel (La) the road over the bishop's tithe allotment behind Newton Fell was to be twelve feet wide with a covering of stones no bigger than a goose's egg, nine inches deep on the crown.[18] The construction of such roads, in place of the previous poorly-surfaced tracks, was one of the major achievements of enclosure, though as late as 1844 the House of Commons Select Committee considered that some enclosure road networks were less well laid out than they might have been and believed that more skilled engineers were needed.[19]

New roads required adequate drainage and road-making accounts indicate that a good deal of attention and expense was sometimes involved in making culverts. In addition, especially in marshy lowlands like the Lyth valley (We) commissioners might have to provide a number of bridges. In Cartmel (La) the provision of such bridges, in place of unsafe fords and slippery stepping stones was seen as one of the most useful aspects of enclosure.[20] The culverts and bridges built for the enclosure commissioners by local labour tend to be sturdy rather than stylish, with the road being carried over the stream on flat slabs or by a simple arch (Figure 27). The cost of constructing both culverts and

Figure 27: An enclosure road above Dent narrows in to reduce the expense of building a culvert.

bridges could be reduced by narrowing the width of the road but in order to avoid having the road surface drop too abruptly when crossing small incised streams a V-shaped wedge of drystone walling, sometimes a dozen feet high, might have to be used to fill in the space (Figure 28). It is no surprise then that the construction of bridges could greatly add to the cost of road-making (Figure 29).

Figure 28: A culvert and massive embankment carry this enclosure road at Skelwyth over a small stream.

Figure 29: Plain and functional: a bridge on an enclosure road above Dent.

On the debit side, while enclosure may have created a greatly improved network of local roads, it also brought a drastic curtailment of rights of access in the areas between them. In a great many townships there is a dense network of tracks and paths recognised as public rights of way among the ancient enclosures but very few through the later allotments (Figure 30).

Figure 30: A rare example of a footpath through the Strickland Roger enclosures.

Many commons had peat mosses where commoners had rights of turbary, or peat cutting, and sometimes rights to cut turf or bracken. Turbaries had to be treated separately so that allotment holders also received a 'moss dale' where they could cut peat. These usually show up on award maps as relatively small areas divided into large numbers of narrow rectangular strips. The owners of moss dales in Woundale, on the Troutbeck (We) enclosure of 1840 were required to replace the turves once peat had been cut on their strips, and to avoid digging them in such a way as to leave holes which might fill with water and cause a hazard. The problem was that these turbary areas were quite small and could be quickly worked out. The entire peat moss might be reclaimed in time; at Brampton (We) the farm of High Moor stands on land which the commissioners allocated for peat cutting. Some turbaries on enclosed land were of little benefit because of their remoteness. On Leck Fell (La) the cottagers, without horses and carts, and even most of the farmers who had them, seldom exercised their rights of turbary. The area allotted as turbary was so high and remote and the road to it so bad that the poor people in Leck used coal for fuel, brought from eight miles away, and for kindling peat from a peat moss a dozen miles distant.[21]

3. *Land improvement and land use*

It is not necessarily safe to assume, especially with regard to the north west, that enclosure was automatically accompanied by agricultural improvement. In many cases, especially during the Napoleonic Wars, enclosure may merely have involved extending a poor crop rotation on to even poorer land. The process of improving the newly-enclosed land involved drainage where necessary. Commissioners had the power to have existing drainage channels cleared and deepened both on former commons and where they ran through ancient enclosures, to drain newly-enclosed land. Sometimes they required the cutting of new drains to reclaim marshy areas and even the drainage of small tarns as at Scotforth (La). At Martindale (We) both drainage and flood protection for the valley-floor allotments was involved, with material being dredged from the stream bed and piled into protective banks. Sometimes a technique of paring off the heathy surface vegetation and burning it was used. The most important improvement was often a heavy does of lime. 100–160 cartloads containing three bushels each were applied to each acre at a cost of a shilling a load. Lime was widely available in the Lune and Eden valleys, Cartmel, Furness and west Cumbria and small limekilns belonging to individual farms are still a common sight on or adjoining the newly-enclosed land. In the upper Eden and Lune valleys the lime was burnt using coal brought by packhorse from the collieries on Stainmore, but in areas where coal was less easily obtained peat could be used as a fuel. Another basic improvement was removing stones from the fields. Sometimes these could be absorbed by the allotment walls but in some cases the stones were too numerous for this and were piled into clearance heaps. On Leck Fell (We) one of the enclosures has been painstakingly cleared of stones which have been piled into a line of huge cairns (Figure 31). On Hugill Fell (We) in the south eastern Lake District a number of allotments have large clearance heaps; other large examples can be seen on Hampsfield Fell (La).

Figure 31: Clearance heaps of stone in an allotment on Leck Fell.

At best this kind of work could raise the annual rental value of the land from sixpence to one shilling to 20 to 30 shillings per acre. The former cultivation of land enclosed by parliamentary act is usually evident by patterns of ridge-and-furrow ploughing, visible in the modern pasture particularly well with slanting morning or evening sunshine or a light cover of snow. Much, but not necessarily all, of this probably dates from the Napoleonic Wars. From the mid-nineteenth century machinery for mass-producing sections of drainage pipes meant that underground tile-drainage became much cheaper and easier to lay so that ridge and furrow became unnecessary but in places land continued to be ploughed in this way until even later.

An example of the profits of improvement on relatively marginal land was given by the Rev. William Carus Wilson in relation to his father's allotment on Casterton Fell (We). The land, before improvement, was worth about two shillings per acre in rent each year. By turning the higher ground over to grouse moor and sheep pasture, and concentrating on the better-quality lower land, liming it and removing stones, it was now good-quality cattle pasture worth 20 shillings a year in rent.[22] The improvement of enclosed land was not always successful, as we have seen. Writing in 1850, William Rothwell described the large area of enclosed land between the Lune Valley and Hutton Roof (We). Much of the land was then under cultivation but he considered that the work of fencing and improvement has been badly done: the walls were poorly built and the land insufficiently well drained. He considered that, with these defects remedied, the land was better suited to improved pasture than arable.[23] The degree to which allotments appreciated in value after enclosure depended, of course, on how well they were managed and there could be marked differences at a local scale. A letter dating from 1869 relating to the Broughton in Furness (La) enclosure of 1847 stated that 'the value of many of the allotments has increased considerably since the date of the award owing to improvement of the land (and) the erection of buildings while that of others has remained the same or has diminished'.[24] Similar contrasts between adjacent allotments can be seen today. On Newton Fell (La) one of the allotments awarded to the Church, still named 'Bishop's Tithe Allotment' on the OS 1:25,000 map, has been let go and is a tangled mixture of high bracken and prickly scrub with hawthorn and holly bushes being prominent. Yet the adjoining allotment to the north, on similar terrain but under different management, is good-quality cattle pasture.

For poorer-quality land afforestation was an alternative use after enclosure. Bailey and Culley calculated that an area of 1,000 acres (405ha), enclosed with a six-foot high fence, could be planted with 500 larch trees per acre at a total cost of £1,000. Sixty years later this would generate an income of £125,000. Even allowing for the loss of rent for the land as grazing during this period the potential profit was considerable.[25] Afforestation was more likely to be undertaken by the owners of large estates. From 1794 John Christian Curwen began planting larches on his allotments on Claife Heights (La) on the west side of Windermere.[26] It is not always easy to distinguish between commercial and amenity planting. At Lupton (We) the Cragmire Plantation, 82 acres (33ha) of Scots pines, was created between the date of the award in 1848 and the first edition of the OS 6-inch map in 1862 by William Beck on the largest of the nine allotments that he received (Figure 32).

Grouse shooting was an alternative to low-grade pasture or afforestation as use for enclosed land, especially in the Pennines with their gentler terrain and heather moorlands. Grouse could be shot by the lord of a manor on an unenclosed common, but where livestock were being grazed there were clearly problems with competing and conflicting land uses. Shooting was more easily undertaken on an individual allotment. One background influence which encouraged the rise of this sport was the construction of the railway network. The main west-coast line over Shap was completed in 1846, the line over Stainmore to Tebay in 1862 and the Settle–Carlisle line in 1876. All these helped to open up the sporting potential of upland estates in this area. Landscape features associated with grouse shooting included lines of grouse butts; the birds were normally driven from periphery towards the centre of allotments to reduce the chance of their flying on to someone else's property (Figure 33). Shooting

Figure 32: Amenity planting on the Lupton enclosure: the artificial pond may have been created for wildfowling.

Figure 33: Grouse butt on a Leck Fell allotment.

huts or lunch shelters were also provided in more remote areas. The large allotments forming the higher parts of the Leck Fell (La) enclosures were, and still are, used for grouse shooting, with stone-built grouse butts lined with timber and floored with gravel, and two shooting houses, one a rickety corrugated iron structure and the other, at the very head of the valley, a low, partly sunken stone structure (Figure 34). Also on Leck Fell a small circular pond is marked on maps as a duck shoot. A slightly larger

Figure 34: Shooting hut on Leck Fell.

artificial lake in the Cragmire plantation, Lupton (We), may also have been created for wildfowling.

4. *New farmsteads*

New farmsteads were a common feature of parliamentary-enclosure landscapes. In a great many cases allotments allocated to customary tenants and small proprietors were annexed to existing holdings and commissioners took a great deal of trouble to ensure, as far as was possible, that the allotments were continuous to existing property. In the process some small farms had their areas substantially increased. At Dalston (Cu) in 1805 enclosure raised average holding size from 33.75 acres to 52 acres (14 to 21ha).[27] In some cases the addition of land to existing farms led to the construction of new outbuildings, as at Brackenthwaite on the edge of Yealand Redmayne (La) common, where the original outbuildings were supplemented by an additional set on the opposite side of the road marking the boundary of the former common. In some cases field barns (Figure 35) or, as north of Shap (We), whole sets of outbuildings (Figure 36) were constructed after enclosure to maximise the efficient use of more distant allotments. Common House (NY 355465) on land awarded to the Rose estate under the Dalston award incorporated a cottage as well as outbuildings to allow the land to be worked efficiently.[28] When larger blocks of land were allotted, especially

Figure 35: Field barn on an allotment at King's Meaburn.

Figure 36: A complete set of outbuildings near Shap.

to manorial lords, or to the church as tithe allotments, or when substantial areas were sold by commissioners to cover the costs of enclosure, opportunities for creating new farms arose. It was unusual to build new farmsteads where the land was very high lying. Leck Fell House and Bullpot Farm above Casterton (We) were exceptions (Figure 37). But on lower moors on the margins of the fells a considerable number of new farms were created, mainly in the late eighteenth century and during the Napoleonic Wars. At Dalston (Cu) five farms ranging from 63 to 263 acres (25 to 106ha) were created.[29] On the Skelton enclosure of 1769, 13 new farms varying in size from 40 to 315 acres (16 to 127ha) were established, accounting for over 1,640 of the 5,000 acres (663 of 2,023ha) enclosed.[30] Sometimes allotments from different townships were amalgamated to create a new farm. In the Reagill (We) award of 1813 the Earl of Lonsdale received a 156-acre (63ha) block on the margins of the township. To this was added an adjacent block of 178 acres (72ha) when the neighbouring township of Newby was enclosed in 1820. A new farmstead, Wintertarn, was built central to this new combined area of land (Map 9). Some farms had more varied histories: the farmhouse at Clickham, on the Brampton (We) enclosure of 1772, looks late eighteenth century in style but is marked as the Dun Cow Inn on the first edition of the OS 6-inch map of 1862. When a number of new farms

Figure 37: Leck Fell House; an unusually high-lying enclosure-period farmstead.

Map 9: The creation of a new farm at Wintertarn on the Reagill enclosure involving land acquired by different means. Map drawn by Chris Beacock.

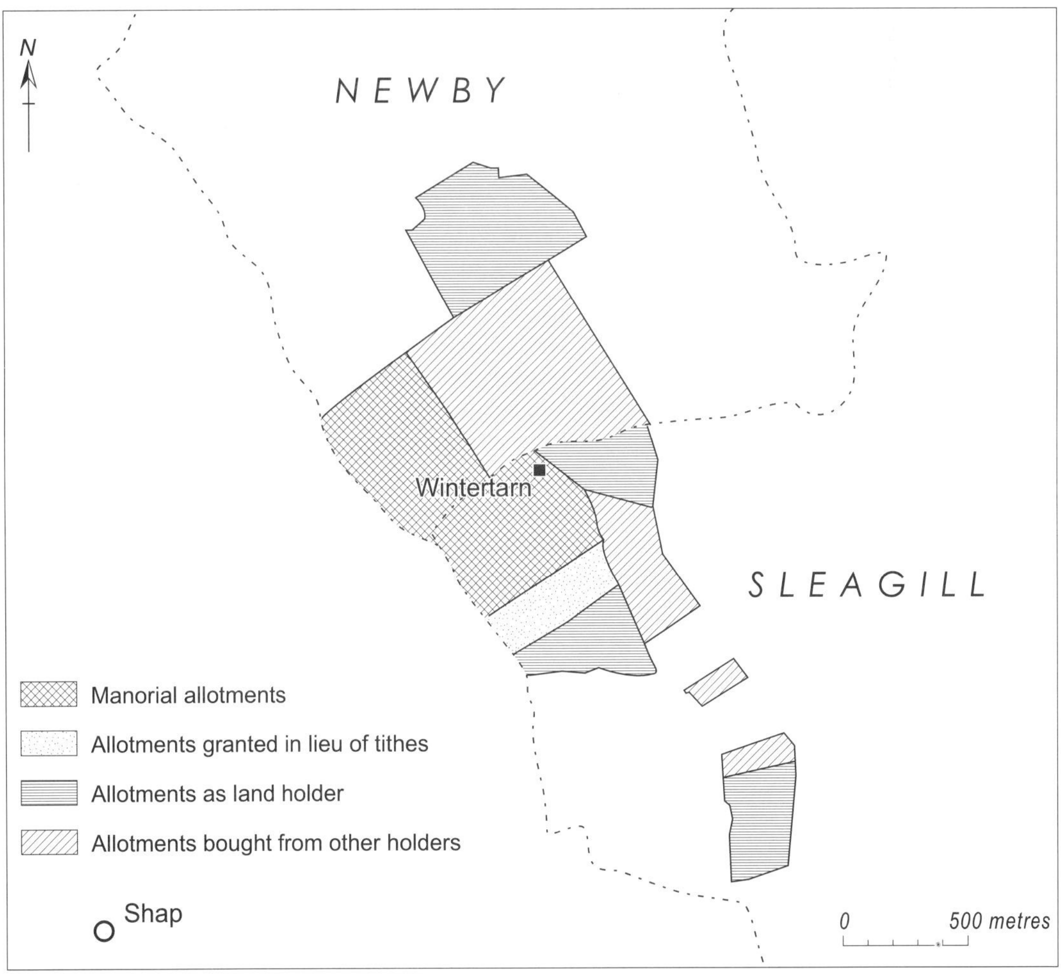

Figure 38: New farm on the Great Ormside enclosure of 1772.

were created on a former common at the same period they often have a similarity of style, as on the Great Ormside (We) enclosure of 1772 (Figure 38).

Some of the new farms were selected for praise by early nineteenth-century agricultural writers. Flan Hill, on the Ulverston enclosure (La), described as 'a romantic little waste land farm of 57 acres (23ha)' had by 1815 39 acres (16ha) under cultivation with a rotation of cereals, green crops and grass. The nearby farm of Rosset, of 68 acres (27.5ha) also provided a model of its kind.[31] Some of the new farmsteads, established in a mood of optimism, have failed to survive the late nineteenth century agricultural depression and twentieth-century farm amalgamation. The steading of Annfield, on the edge of the Leck Fell (La) enclosure, was marked on the OS map in 1847 but today all that remains are ruins, just sufficient to show the L-shaped layout of the buildings. A more recent desertion is Rawbusk, remote and awkwardly located on the floor of the narrow Eller Gill valley, adjoining the Ellergill Cowbound (We) enclosure of 1867. Here the house and outbuildings are still roofed (Figure 39). Even sadder, in some respects, is the eloquently-named Moorcock Hall, 260 metres up on the north-facing edge of Bowland, above the Lune valley on the Claughton (La) enclosure. Here efforts were made to create a stylish farmstead with a Georgian façade and a substantial set of outbuildings on either side. Today all that remains is a roofless shell, the brick chimney stacks lying among the remains of rafters and floorboards, sandwiched between the swish of the wind turbines on Caton Moor and the creak of the ropeway for the Claughton brickworks (Figure 40). At Eastview, the only new steading on the Strickland Roger (We) enclosure, a massive stone embankment up to four metres high had to be built on

Figure 39: Abandoned farm of Rawbusk on the Ellergill Cowbound enclosure of 1867.

Figure 40: Moorcock Hall on the Claughton enclosure.

the steep hillside to provide a sufficiently big platform for the farmhouse and outbuildings to stand on. The buildings now stand roofless and abandoned, mute testimony to the changed circumstances of modern farming (Figure 41).

Names such as Heights, Hill Top, Moor House and Newlands reflect the origins of some of the farms. Occasionally names are more topical; on the enclosures just south of Cockermouth, dating from around 1824, new farms named Wellington (NY108296) and Waterloo (NY118288) are clear reminders of the period when they were created. Mostly, though, the new farms have more prosaic names derived from local topographic features or the surnames of the first occupiers. Documentation relating to such new farms is hard to track down but an advertisement survives for the construction of a farmstead on an allotment at Hutton Roof (We). A house, barn, shippon and stable were required, built to a pre-determined plan.[32]

The conversion of land from common pasture to individual ownership allowed proprietors a wide range of options regarding land use, not all of which were agricultural. Large-scale quarrying for slate, as at the head of Longsleddale, or for limestone, as on Hutton Roof, was one option. Coal mining was another, especially in west Cumberland. At Claughton (La) in the Lune valley a brickworks was set up around 1887 and is still functioning.[33] At Strickland Roger (We) the switch to individual

Figure 41: Eastview, the only new farm on the Strickland Roger enclosure, now abandoned.

Figure 42: Artificial tarn at Gurnal Dubbs on the Strickland Roger enclosure, supplying water to Burneside but also creating a trout fishery.

ownership allowed valleys to be dammed to create sources of water power for the paper mills in nearby Burneside, the artificial tarns providing, in addition trout fisheries (Figure 42). The conversion of land from communal to individual ownership allowed the construction of a range of monuments, towers and follies, like the Hospice, a shelter and outlook tower on top of Hampsfield Fell (La) (Figure 43) or the ruined tower on Dixon Heights above Lindale (La). Equally curious is the Second World War pillbox apparently guarding Newton Fell (La) from Nazi invasion.

Figure 43: The Hospice, Hampsfield Fell, a shelter and outlook tower.

Notes

1. J. Clarke, *A Survey of the Lakes of Cumberland, Westmorland and Lancashire* (1787), p.5.
2. CRO Kendal HH/119.
3. A.J.L. Winchester, *The Harvest of the Hills* (Edinburgh University Press, 2000), pp.62–64.
4. CRO Kendal WQR/I/41.
5. A. B. Humphries, 'Agrarian Change in East Cumberland, 1750–1900', Unpublished M.Phil.Thesis, University of Lancaster, 1993, p.664.
6. CRO (Kendal) WDX/100.
7. R.W. Dickson, *General View of the Agriculture of Lancashire* (1815), p.200.
8. J.T. Relph, *Chronicles of Crosby Ravensworth* (1992), p.43.
9. CRO (Kendal) WDX 14/1.
10. LRO DDX/3/11–13.
11. Humphries, Agrarian Change, p.157.
12. CRO (Kendal) WDB/35/838.
13. Winchester, *Harvest of the Hills*, p.69.
14. B.P. Hindle, *Roads and Trackways in the Lake District* (Moorland, 1984), p.172.
15. For example, CRO (Kendal) WPR/24/Z5.
16. F.W. Garnett, *Westmorland Agriculture 1800–1900* (Titus Wilson, 1912), p.53.
17. J. Turnbull, 'An Economic and Social Study of Orton (Westmorland) Between 1650 and 1850', Unpublished Diploma in Local History Dissertation, University of Liverpool and Lancaster, 1984, p.32.
18. J. Stockdale, *Annals of Cartmel* (Kitchin, 1872), p.346.
19. Select Committee on Commons Inclosure 1844, Command Paper 583, vol 5, p.19.
20. Stockdale, *Annals of Cartmel*, p.326.
21. Select Committee on Inclosure, vol 5, p.128.
22. *Ibid*, p.125.
23. W. Rothwell, *Report on the Agriculture of the County of Lancaster* (1850), p.22.
24. CRO (Barrow) BD17/19.
25. J. Bailey & G. Culley, *General View of the Agriculture of Northumberland, Cumberland and Westmorland* (Nicol, 1805), pp.284–87.
26. R. Millward & A. Robinson, *The Lake District* (Eyre & Spottiswoode, 1970), p.55.
27. Humphries, *Agrarian Change*, pp.191–195.
28. *Ibid.*, pp.672–3.
29. *Ibid.*, p.191.
30. *Ibid.*, pp.167–8.
31. Dickson, *General View*, pp.227, 240.
32. CRO (Kendal) WD/PP Box 2 no 34.
33. J.W.A. Price, *The Industrial Architecture of the Lune Valley* (CNWRS, 1983), p.80.

CHAPTER SEVEN

The social impacts of enclosure

Parliamentary enclosure has been seen by many historians as a process by which wealthy landowners could oppress smallholders, cottagers and squatters.[1] By removing their varied rights to the use of common land, landowners in lowland England could alter the structure of rural society, removing the partial independence that smallholding labourers enjoyed through access to common rights, including the ability to keep a cow, fatten pigs, and collect fuel and other resources. As a result men were forced into full-time paid labour which, especially in arable areas, had seasonal slack periods during which labouring families often had to apply for poor relief. Although the creation of the new enclosed landscape; planting the hedges, digging the ditches and making the new roads, might create a temporary burst of employment such work was often done by jobbing gangs of labourers from outside the immediate area. The rationalisation of labour which accompanied enclosure sometimes led to a shift from farming to cottage industry but in other cases it produced out-migration and depopulation. In such circumstances, enclosure has been seen as a powerful weapon in the extermination of the English peasantry.[2] To what extent was this the case in the north west and what were the impacts of enclosure on rural society there?

Much of the impact of enclosure depends on the initial structure of rural society. The picture for north west England is far from clear. As we have seen, a high proportion of the farmers in Cumberland and Westmorland were customary tenants whose rights to a share of enclosed land seem to have been widely acknowledged by manorial lords and other proprietors. Many of these customary tenants occupied quite small farms. But, at a lower level, how large was the class of cottagers who might have worked part-time for larger farmers and to what extent were their rights acknowledged by the enclosure commissioners? We know from the enclosure awards that squatters who had occupied plots on a common for less than 20 years were not recognised as having common rights but it is far from clear how numerous such people were. In addition, many of them were clearly farmers trying to add to their existing holdings rather than poor cottagers. Establishing the size and significance of those groups at the lower levels of society is difficult because they are not recorded reliably and unambiguously in most historical sources. Some of these, like the land tax returns, are notoriously unreliable and difficult to interpret[3] or, like the census enumerators' books, are too late in date for most enclosures. However, the Westmorland Census of 1787 shows for some parishes that relatively few people were listed simply as labourers or cottagers.[4] More numerous were farm servants, young men and women in their late teens or twenties, living in the household of farmers as part of a life-cycle phase which usually ended at marriage. In many cases, presumably, where their fathers were customary tenants they would eventually inherit the holding or, if younger sons, they might eventually save enough money to lease land of their own. Compared with areas further south farms were small, using mainly family labour, while access to land seems to have been more widespread.

An point to emphasise is that with the parliamentary enclosure of open field arable land, once deductions had been made for the lord of the manor's and the tithe holder's shares, landowners got back less land than they had started with, albeit concentrated more efficiently in a block rather than a scatter of strips and parcels. With the enclosure of upland commons landowners received more land rather than less, sometimes quite a lot more. Where enclosure awards list the amounts of land on which the award of allotments were based it is possible to calculate by how much existing holdings increased in size as a result of enclosure. The new allotments frequently added 30, 50 or even 100 per cent to the size of existing holdings. In proportional terms smallholders often did better than larger landowners.

Table 9 shows that in manors with smaller lowland commons, like Colby, Maulds Meaburn and Newbiggin, there were relatively small average increases in holding size (though the quality of the land in the

Table 9. Average increase in holding size with enclosure in Westmorland (%).

	Date	%
Asby Mask	1855	70
Asby Winderwath	1874	65
Colby	1854	28
Grayrigg	1868	75
Great Musgrave	1859	59
Hillbeck	1859	136
Kirkby Stephen	1855	85
Lambrigg	1886	37
Little Musgrave	1853	41
Newbiggin	1850	55
Maulds Meaburn	1858	37
Smardale	1849	135
Waitby	1855	72

(Source: Enclosure awards)

new allotments may have been relatively high) while in those with large upland commons such as Hillbeck, Kirkby Stephen and Smardale there were greater proportional increases. On the basis of such increases in holding sizes, with the widespread conversion of rough pasture to improved grazing and sometimes arable, enclosure in the north west should generally have led to an increased demand for labour. Most late eighteenth and early nineteenth-century writers on agricultural improvement certainly thought so. William Carus Wilson, appearing before the House of Commons Select Committee in 1844 and speaking of townships in the parishes of Kendal and Kirkby Lonsdale of which he had direct experience, claimed that the situation regarding cottagers was very different in the north of England compared with the south. There were far fewer of them, their rights were taken into account by the commissioners and enclosure provided more work for them in both the short and longer term.[5] This seems particularly likely where the area enclosed was large and included a number of new farms, as with Inglewood Forest (Cu).

The official census from 1801 onwards presents a generally favourable picture of the impact of enclosure on population. In a few cases, such as Edenhall, Isell and Great Salkeld in Cumberland in 1821, the census actually explains that a rise in population was due to enclosure. The rises in population from 1811 to 1821 in these three cases were 90, 19 and 39 per cent respectively.

However, not everyone thought that enclosure was an advantage to the poorest people. While most writers emphasised how enclosure increased local food supplies and generated more demand for labour, tending to increase the population, some associated enclosure with depopulation, Hutchinson, writing in 1794 of the enclosure of Skelton (Cu) in 1769, claimed that population had fallen after enclosure as many cottagers had been forced to leave.[6] Stockdale, in his history of Cartmel, considered that enclosure there in the early nineteenth century was not at all beneficial to cottagers and smallholders, and led to out-migration and a loss of population in some townships. He claimed that numbers of smallholders paying the land tax at the lowest rate fell by 20 per cent between 1796 and 1811.[7] Marshall also suggested that enclosure was a direct cause of the depopulation that occurred in some Cartmel townships at this period.[8] As we saw in Chapter 4 there is evidence that the proceedings of the Cartmel enclosure may not have been as favourable to the rights of smallholders and cottagers as other awards within the region. In some cases, where small tenants did receive allotments they may have been located too far from their homes to be useful.[9] It is important to note, however, that other changes not necessarily directly linked to enclosure, such as a slow trend towards the amalgamation of farms, changing patterns of rural industry and migration to industrial centres in south Lancashire and the north east, were also likely to have affected rural population levels.

It is hard to establish the extent to which people with only a cottage and garden had their use of the commons recognised so that they received allotments, and to what degree the allotments they were awarded made up for the loss of various common rights. It has been suggested that in the early eighteenth century manorial courts generally accepted that cottagers had some sort of right to the use of upland commons but that there was an increasing hardening of attitudes against this by the end of the century.[10] Doubtless, too, the degree to which cottagers had recognised rights varied from one manor to another.

Enclosure, through the sale of allotments and the purchase of land disposed of to meet expenses, gave existing landowners the chance to increase the sizes of their holdings and allowed outsiders to buy land. Some allotment holders also sold out their common rights before the award was made. There was considerable variation between enclosures regarding how land was sold to meet costs. Sometimes land went mostly to existing allotment holders, allowing them to expand their estates even more. At Reagill (We) John Bland received allotments of 15 and 16 acres (6 & 6.5ha) but added to them another 38 acres (15ha) bought from the commissioners. The land was chosen to form a compact block on which the new farmstead of Wyebourne was built. Sometimes the land was sold off in small lots so that tradesmen and labourers could purchase it, as happened at Bolton and Little Musgrave (We). Sometimes the land was sold in a single large block, as with Casterton (We) where 1,325 acres (536ha) were sold to Joseph Gibson. Many people from outside the community took the opportunity of purchasing land. At Over Staveley (We) buyers included a manufacturer from Shropshire and a man from Sussex as well as, more locally, the owner of Fell Foot bobbin mill. Overall, however, it was local people who predominated as purchasers

Although there were undoubledly changes in patterns of landownership as a result of enclosure it is the underlying continuity in rural society within the north west which is most striking. The pattern of small farms using family labour and farm servants continued throughout the nineteenth century into the twentieth. Enclosure was one element, along with improved transport and the development of more distant markets, which gradually made rural society more prosperous without altering it drastically.

Notes

1. For example, see; J. Hammond & B. Hammond, *The Village Labourer* (Longmans 1912); J.D. Chambers & G.E. Mingay, *The Agricultural Revolution 1750–1880* (Batsford 1966).

2. K.D.M. Snell, *Annals of the Labouring Poor: social change and agrarian England, 1660–1900* (Cambridge University Press 1985), pp.138–223.
3. Snell, *Annals*, pp.139–41.
4. L. Ashcroft, *Vital Statistics. The Westmorland 'Census' of 1787* (Curwen Archive Trust, 1992).
5. Select Committee on Commons Inclosure, 1844, Command Paper 583, vol 5, p.130.
6. W. Hutchinson, *The History of the County of Cumberland and some Places Adjacent.* (Jollie, 1794) vol 1, p.514.
7. J. Stockdale, *Annals of Cartmel* (Kitchin 1782), p.257.
8. J.D. Marshall, *Furness in the Industrial Revolution, an economic history of Furness 1711–1900* (Barrow-in-Furness Libraries, 1958).
9. N. Gregson, 'Continuity in agrarian organisation in north-west England, 1100–1800', Unpublished PhD. Thesis, University of Durham, 1984, p. 213.
10. C.E. Searle, 'Customary tenants and the enclosure of the Cumbrian commons', *Northern History* 29 (1993), pp.126–53.

Conclusion

Early twentieth-century English agricultural historians tended to over-emphasise the importance of parliamentary enclosure suggesting that, as a result of it, most of the English landscape dated no further back than the eighteenth century. Since then landscape historians have demonstrated that much of our landscape is a good deal older than this. Within the north west the impact of parliamentary enclosure, especially in the uplands, is patchy and variable. In addition, the extent of change is sometimes relatively limited, especially as regards land use. In Gressingham parish (La), a local historian writing early in the twentieth century, commented that over a century after enclosure some of the allotments did not look any different from their original condition as open moorland.[1] Sometimes the land use changes brought about by enclosure appear minimal: Figure 44 shows the boundary of the Dent (Yo) enclosure and Barbon common but there is no obvious difference on either side of the boundary in terms of the vegetation cover. On the other hand along boundaries such as that between Orton and Crosby Ravensworth (We) the contrast between improved pasture in the enclosed land of the former and the unimproved open common of the latter is striking (Figure 8).

Where parliamentary enclosure occurred it not only changed the landscape but sometimes precipitated further changes. From the window of my office at Lancaster University I can look towards the Bowland fells over a landscape which, in the last 200 years, has been totally remodelled three times. At the end of the eighteenth century it was an area of common pasture, part of Scotforth Moor. After enclosure in around 1809 it became farmland. In the late nineteenth century it was converted into a sporting estate with the construction of Bailrigg House. From the 1960s it has developed as a university campus. Much of the present woodland originated as plantings on the Bailrigg estate but the parliamentary enclosure hedgerows are still evident.

Parliamentary enclosure has been described as one of the most important exercises in landscape planning of any era.[2] Nevertheless, it was very much the product of local decision making and is, as a result, sporadic in its distribution. Much unenclosed land remains; it is still possible to walk from one side of Westmorland to the other without

Figure 44: The boundary between the Dent enclosures (right) and Barbon common (left): can you spot any difference?

leaving common land. Just over 100,000 acres (4,047ha) of common land were enclosed in Westmorland yet over 129,000 acres (52,206ha) remain open.[3] On the other hand, over extensive areas of the uplands and moorlands, the character of the modern landscape with its regular fields, straight roads and farmsteads still reflects the decisions that were made by the enclosure commissioners. This comes out most dramatically in Inglewood Forest (Cu) where, in addition to the 28,000 acre (11,332ha) block enclosed from 1819 there are other large areas of enclosure such as Skelton (5,000 acres 2,024ha), Castle Sowerby (5,000 acres 2,024ha) and Sebergham (2,896 acres 1,172ha). In this area you can drive for miles along ruler-straight roads, switchbacking across the gently undulating terrain. There are few villages and most of the farmsteads are set back from the road in the centre of their allotments; a landscape which is lonely, monotonous but very distinctive. If the scale and impact of parliamentary enclosure has sometimes been exaggerated it is nevertheless worth remembering the comments of some contemporary commentators who stress the amount of the landscape change involved. John Housman, writing of the country north of Penrith in 1821, described how the area was formerly an extensive common eight or nine miles long with a ridge of barren hills in the middle (the sandstone ridge running north from Penrith Beacon). At the time of writing, after enclosure, it was characterised by 'woods, farm houses and rich crops of corn where furze and ling once principally prevailed',[4] though today quite extensive areas are planted with conifers (Figure 45). Garnett, writing about Westmorland, emphasised how enclosure hastened the development of agriculture in the county even more than its strongest advocates had believed, carrying farming on a wave for the first 50 or 60 years of the nineteenth century.[5]

The names and the work of the enclosure commissioners have generally been forgotten though a plaque on the wall of the Cavendish Arms in Cartmel (La) commemorates the holding there of the public meetings concerning enclosure, while another plaque, fixed to a reused

Figure 45: Enclosure landscape on the sandstone ridge north of Penrith.

gatepost, commemorates the granting of the Strickland Roger (We) recreation allotment in 1853 (Figure 46). The landscape they created has often changed relatively little since their time. Parliamentary enclosure landscapes among the fells of north west England are increasingly poorly maintained today. Choked drains and broken culverts have caused sedges to invade the pastures and the flooding of enclosure roads (Figure 47).

Figure 46: Plaque commemorating the granting of the recreation allotment to the people of Strickland Roger.

Figure 47: Enclosure road on Wansfell, overgrown and badly drained.

Walls, especially on internal boundaries, receive little or no maintenance and are often in a tumbled state. With the recent crisis in hill farming, especially following the foot-and-mouth outbreak, land use in the uplands is likely to become even less intensive and landscape maintenance, unless supported by grants such as those through the Environmentally Sensitive Areas scheme, even further reduced. The history of the enclosure process, and how it was carried out, is scarcely known to many of the farmers who work the land today. Walking the roads and footpaths laid out by the enclosure surveyors has not only helped to keep me fit; it has prompted some interesting conversations with farmers. Appearing outside a farm gate with a clipboard, I have sometimes been taken, initially, as someone from the council making unspecified checks. Having established the real purpose of my visit, I have often been asked to tell the story of the local enclosure and of the people behind it. I have now told the story to a wider audience in the hope of passing on something of my own interest and enthusiasm. Next time you go out on the fells I hope that you will look at the landscape around you with fresh interest and insight.

Notes

1. W.H. Chippindall, *History of the Township of Gressingham* (1919), p.103.
2. M.E. Turner, 'The landscape of Parliamentary Enclosure' in M. Reed (ed), *Discovering Past Landscapes* (Croom Helm, 1984), p.135.
3. W.G. Hoskins & L.S. Stamp, *The Common Lands of England and Wales* (Collins, 1963), Appendix A.
4. J. Housman, *A Descriptive Tour and Guide to the Lakes, Caves, Mountains and other Natural Curiosities in Cumberland, Westmoreland, Lancashire and a part of the West Riding of Yorkshire* (Jollie, 1821), p.57.
5. F.W. Garnett, *Westmorland Agriculture, 1800–1900* (Titus Wilson, 1912), p.30.

A guide to further reading

The standard work on parliamentary enclosure, M. Turner, *English Parliamentary Enclosure: its historical geography and economic history* (Dawson, 1980), provides a dense, statistically heavyweight introduction to the topic at a national scale. G.E. Mingay, *Parliamentary enclosure in England: an introduction to its causes, incidence and impact, 1750–1850* (Longman, 1998) is more readable.

For background on the pre-enclosure landscape in the north west, A.J.L. Winchester, *The Harvest of the Hills: rural life in Northern England and the Scottish Borders, 1400–1700* (Edinburgh University Press, 2000) is invaluable, and his *Landscape and Society in Medieval Cumbria* (John Donald, 1987) although covering an earlier period is also useful. For earlier field systems see; G. Elliott, 'Field systems of North West England' in A.R.H. Baker & R.A. Butlin (eds.), *Studies of Field Systems in the British Isles* (Cambridge University Press, 1973), pp.41–92. On the social side see A.B. Appleby, *Famine in Tudor and Stuart England* (Liverpool University Press, 1978).

The background to parliamentary enclosure in Cumbria has been discussed in a trio of articles by C.E. Searle: 'Custom, Class Conflict and Agrarian Capitalism: The Cumbrian Customary Economy in the Eighteenth Century', *Past and Present* 110 (1986), pp.106–33; 'Customary tenants and the enclosure of the Cumbrian commons', *Northern History* 29 (1993), pp.126–53, and 'Cumbria's parliamentary enclosure movement: a comparative study in rural quiescence', *TCWAAS* Second Series 95 (1995), pp.247–69.

For recent thinking on the social impact of enclosure in midland and southern England see K.D.M. Snell, *Annals of the Labouring Poor: social change and agrarian England, 1660–1900* (Cambridge University Press, 1985) and J.M. Neeson, *Commoners: common right, enclosure and social change in England 1700–1820* (Cambridge University Press, 1993). For rural society towards the end of the enclosure era see M.E. Shepherd, 'The small owner in Cumbria c.1840–1910: a case study from the upper Eden valley', *Northern History* 35 (1999), pp.161–84.

Printed contemporary, or near-contemporary sources which include interesting material on enclosure include J. Stockdale, *Annals of Cartmel* (Kitchin, 1872) and the proceedings of the House of Commons Select

Committee on Commons Inclosure (1844), Command Paper 583. The article by Crayston Webster, himself an enclosure valuer, 'The farming of Westmorland', *Journal of the Royal Society of Agriculture of England* 2nd ser., 4 (1868), pp.1–39 is especially informative while there is also a good deal of material in F.W. Garnett, *Westmorland Farming, 1800–1900* (Titus Wilson, 1912).

Anyone wishing to work with enclosure records should read S. Hollowell, *Enclosure Records for Historians* (Phillimore, 2000). The enclosure awards, with their maps, are fully indexed and readily available at the record offices in Carlisle (covering the old County of Cumberland), Barrow (covering Furness and Cartmel), Kendal (covering the former Westmorland) and Preston (Lancashire south of the Sands). A list of all known awards is given in W.E. Tate, *A Domesday of English enclosure acts and awards* (University of Reading, 1978).

For exploring parliamentary enclosure landscapes on foot, the OS 1:25,000 maps showing rights of way are essential. The first edition 6-inch to the mile (1:10,560) survey, dating from the late 1840s in Lancashire and the 1860s in Cumbria, provides an excellent record of the immediate post-enclosure landscape and is available on www.old-maps.co.uk.

Index